Financial Policies and Everyday Life

Savak Sohrab Tarapore, B.A. (Honours) Economics, Sheffield University (1958), M.Sc (Economics), London University (1960) and Doctor of Laws, honoris causa, Sheffield University (1996), was a career central banker. He joined the RBI in 1961 as Research Officer and retired as Deputy Governor in September 1996. Since his retirement, he was Chairman of a number of official committees: Capital Account Convertibility (1997), Inquiry into the Affairs of the Unit Trust of India (2001), Procedures and Performance Audit of Public Services (2003-04) and Fuller Capital Account Convertibility (2006). He was a Member of the Committee on Banking Sector Reforms (1998), Advisory Group on Transparency in Monetary and Financial Policies (2000) and the RBI Technical Advisory Committee on Monetary Policy (2004-2008). He was Chairman of the Advisory Board on Banking, Commercial and Financial Frauds (1997-2001) and Chairman, Discount and Finance House of India (2001-2004). He was successively a columnist for the Business Standard, The Financial Express and the Divya Bhaskar and is currently a columnist for the Hindu Business Line. He is a member of the Court of Governors of the Administrative Staff College of India and a trustee of the N.M. Wadia Charities. He has published five books on financial policies.

Financial Policies and Everyday Life

The Indian Context

S.S Tarapore

ACADEMIC FOUNDATION
NEW DELHI

First published in 2010
by

ACADEMIC FOUNDATION
4772-73 / 23 Bharat Ram Road, (23 Ansari Road),
Darya Ganj, New Delhi - 110 002 (India).
Phones : 23245001 / 02 / 03 / 04.
Fax : +91-11-23245005.
E-mail : books@academicfoundation.com
www. academicfoundation.com

Cataloging in Publication Data--DK
Courtesy: D.K. Agencies (P) Ltd. <docinfo@dkagencies.com>

S.S. Tarapore.
Financial Policies and Everyday Life: The Indian Context/
S.S. Tarapore.
p. cm.
Includes bibliographical references (p.).
Includes index.
ISBN 13: 9788171888061
ISBN 10: 8171888062

1. People with social disabilities--Government policy--India.
2. Reverse discrimination--India. I. Title.

DDC 305.5680954 22

Typeset by Italics India, New Delhi.
Printed and bound in India.

To
My Grandchildren

Riya, Neil and Kyra

Contents

II

III

IV

V

VI

VII

VIII

Preface

This volume is a collection of columns in the *Divya Bhaskar*, a widely circulating Gujarati daily. It is increasingly being felt that for a meaningful debate on economic and financial policies the issues need to be communicated in regional languages so as to reach out to the masses. This volume presents, for the first time, these articles for the English speaking readers.

While these articles have been written from the viewpoint of the general reader, they have also been provocative enough for policymakers and others to read.

I am deeply indebted to Mr. Girish Agarwal, Director of the Bhaskar Group for having graciously invited me to write a column in the *Divya Bhaskar*. Mr. Anil Patel, in charge of the Commercial Section of the *Divya Bhaskar* (Ahmedabad) and Mr. Jayesh Chitalia (of the Mumbai office) went beyond the call of duty to help ensure efficient production of the column.

My daughter Anjalee not only helped me in producing the column but was also a trenchant critic, evaluating the drafts to make them reader friendly.

S.S. Tarapore

Introduction

This collection of 70 short articles *Financial Policies and Everyday Life* is directed to the general reader who has a stake in how financial policies are formulated and their implications for the *aam aadmi*.

The book is divided into eight parts.

Part I attempts to set out the essence of monetary policy from the viewpoint of the common person who needs to be aware of how the Reserve Bank of India (RBI) monetary policy impinges on individuals. The writer attempts to explain the advantages of early monetary policy action before the economy goes through the inevitable cyclical downturn. It is true that the writer comes out as an unabashed admirer of Governor Dr. Y.V. Reddy, yet there are economists in the RBI who were occasionally livid at the trenchant criticism when the writer disagreed with the RBI. On the whole, the writer's assessment was that the RBI had handled monetary policy deftly through difficult times.

Part II relates to the implications of interest rate policy as it affects the common person and the writer endeavours to provide strategies for dealing with changes in policies.

Part III deals with the difficult problem of the fisc, given the multiple objectives. The art of good management is to curtail fiscal deficits in good times and to expand during the downturn of activity. The writer is supportive of the Fiscal Responsibility and Budget Management Act, though he stresses the need to ensure fiscal transparency.

Part IV focuses on the problems of small savers and the leitmotif of the writer's thoughts is that the small saver is short-changed by iniquitous fiscal policies.

Part V on banking stays away from the commanding heights of banking problems from a macro perspective and instead discusses, at length, the various measures put in place to ensure that the rights of small customers are safeguarded. In fact, the writer believes that of the many achievements of Dr. Reddy during his Governorship, concrete action to ensure that small customers are provided their legitimate dues will, in a historical context, be considered as Dr. Reddy's enduring contribution.

Part VI deals with external sector issues. The writer urges the authorities to take early action before the tsunami of capital inflows as well as the exodus of capital. The writer is a supporter of the RBI's exchange rate management and he does not agree with critics who argue for free play for the exchange rate.

Part VII clearly brings out that the writer is a gold buff. According to him, the country is losing heavily because of the passive policy on gold, both in terms of the official reserves and also from the viewpoint of the individual holder of gold. The writer's view is that by giving up the idea of a Gold Bank in 1992, even after announcing it in the budget of 1992 that such a bank would be set up, was most unfortunate and the country will rue at this lapse.

Part VIII deals with three other issues which are distinct and separate *viz.,* Corporate Social Responsibility, RBI Balance Sheet and the Tragedy of Pulses all of which are still very burning issues.

The writer recognises that the general reader could be baffled by the jargon but it is his belief that it is the duty of economists/writers to endeavour to reach out and assist the common person to comprehend the essence of financial policies to facilitate the taking of considered decisions on their personal finances.

I

1 Monetary Policy

RBI Goes the Chinese Way

The Reserve Bank of India (RBI) Annual Policy Statement for the year 2006-2007 was announced by the Governor Dr. Y.V. Reddy on April 18, 2006 amidst considerable hoopla amongst the media and financial market participants. Unlike in the 1980s, when major policy measures were announced with laconic statements, a distinguishing feature of the Reddy era has been the lucid and comprehensive communication mechanism. Not only are policy changes explained but explanations are given for maintaining the *status quo*. The April 18, 2006 policy statement is a *tour de force* of the internal and external environment in both the real and monetary sectors as a backdrop to the policy stance.

Mervyn King, Governor of the Bank of England recently introduced cricketing terminology to explain central bank actions. It is important for markets to know what kind of a bowler Dr. Reddy is. If he were to bowl immaculately good length balls as Vijay Hazare, the famous Indian cricketer of the 1940s and 1950s, he would not give away runs but then he would be ineffective in taking wickets, or in other words his policies would not have any impact. The skill of Dr. Reddy is that when his policies bite he does not snarl but when he snarls and gives warning signals he does not bite. He mixes up his full tosses, half volleys, good length ball googlies, reverse swing, bumpers and doosras. More importantly, he sometimes bowls a chinaman (a ball that swings away just as the batsman expects it to come right on to the bat). If monetary policies were totally predictable it would become boring. At the same time, Governor Reddy recognises the imperative need for not destabilising markets.

Now, why are we talking about the chinaman? The fact is that while Dr. Reddy refers in his statement to evolving monetary policies in industrial and emerging markets we also need to take a peep at the current Chinese monetary policy to understand Indian monetary policy. China recently decided to stick to a stable monetary policy even though loan growth is accelerating and the banking system is awash with liquidity. Analysts expected the central bank to raise reserve requirements to mop excess liquidity and to raise interest rates to rein in credit growth. The central bank is at pains to assure that any monetary tightening in the future would not impinge on the stock market. The State Council (Cabinet) recognises that money supply was growing too fast and that credit was too loose. The broad money, M2, expansion on a year-on-year basis in March 2006, was 18.8 per cent as against a target of 16 per cent. The concern is that monetary tightening could hurt the high real growth rate. Credit to the property sector could be excessive and there are clear signs of over-lending. The authorities feel an imperative need to increase lending to small businesses and rural borrowers. Banks are providing funds to risky areas (Reuters report in the *Hindu Business Line* April 16, 2006). The Chinese authorities are also aware about the overheating of the economy. Overly fast expansion in credit could result in accelerating inflation, generating economic imbalances and a chaotic economic structure. Bad loans can emerge as a result of the surge in investment which will cause rising cost of raw materials and intermediates while demand for final products could fall and squeeze profits. After all these warnings, the Chinese central bank has opted for an unchanged monetary policy, though it must, in fairness, be said that the central bank stands in readiness for swift action if warranted. It seems that the central banks of China and India have great empathy for each other.

While Governor Reddy has silenced his critics on interest rates, for the time being, he has moved with great alacrity to increase the general provisioning requirements from 0.4 per cent to 1.0 per cent on standard assets for personal loans, capital market exposure, residential housing above Rs. 20 lakh and commercial estate loans. The impact of this measure has been to raise interest rates on loans to these sectors. For housing loans it would perhaps have been better if the RBI had used a loan-asset ratio to tighten measures. The risk weights on exposure to commercial real estate and venture capital funds included for capital market exposure has been raised from 125 per cent to 150 per cent.

The Liquidity Adjustment Facility (LAF) is essentially for short-term adjustments for surpluses and deficits in bank liquidity. Under the present system the RBI absorbs and injects liquidity in unlimited amounts at fixed rates of interest. The RBI could move over to a variable interest LAF with discretion to determine the amount absorbed or injected by the RBI. The LAF should not become a passive instrument in handling liquidity in the system. Furthermore, RBI needs to hone its skills for active open market operations.

In the coming months the RBI will have to be vigilant as the essence of effective monetary management is the undertaking of timely measures. While it is easy to criticise central bank actions, what is important is that we try to understand the stance at a particular point of time—for that we need to read the statement not only line by line but also between the lines.

Divya Bhaskar—May 1, 2006.

2 Need a Cautionary Monetary Policy

In the run up to the monetary policy announcement on April 18, 2006 there will be expectations of release of goodies and fears of adverse action.

In the forefront would be the plea that the Reserve Bank of India (RBI) should ease the policy and release large liquidity into the system. It is claimed that ample liquidity is a prerequisite for continued and higher growth. Inflation nutters, it would be argued, should be ignored and the credit expansion party should be allowed to get merrier. Such an approach cannot be the basis for formulating a responsible monetary policy.

The RBI follows a multiple monetary indicators approach. Individual commentators/analysts would put emphasis on different indicators according to their own proclivities.

First, it is increasingly recognised that there is a real sector cycle wherein there are limits to growth and an economy which overheats and grows at a rate above its optimal potential will face a downturn. The Indian economy has been growing at an unprecedented 8 per cent per annum for the past three years and while there are aspirations for higher rates of growth, a responsible assessment should lead us to understand that we are close to the upper turning point of the real sector cycle. To the extent monetary policy has a role, its proper task is to take appropriate policy action as the economy approaches the upper turning point of the real sector cycle.

Secondly, the Indian economy is more closely integrated with the international economy than hitherto and we can no longer say that Indian interest rates are not connected to international interest rates. Moreover, the real rates of interest need to be higher in emerging markets than in major industrial countries. The US Fed, the European Central Bank and the Bank of Japan, are all in a monetary tightening mode. Given our increased integration with the world economy, there would be destabilising effects if India believes that it can be insulated from changes in international interest rates. To the extent we ignore movements in international interest rates we should be prepared for capital outflows and a depreciation of the exchange rate and acceleration in inflation.

Thirdly, although inflation in India is presently moderate, what is relevant is inflationary expectations. Once inflationary expectations get entrenched, bringing back inflation to tolerable levels involves heavy costs in terms of loss of output and related suffering for the weaker sections of society. Broad money (M3) on a year-on-year basis is increasing at 16.3 per cent while reserve money (money created by RBI) is expanding at 18.3 per cent which is clearly excessive.

Fourthly, although the current account deficit of 3 per cent of GDP is not too alarming, it is yet another indicator that the Indian economy is stretching at the leash. Furthermore, the oil price of US$ 60 plus per barrel is more than transitory and this will have inevitable adverse effects on the Indian economy.

Fifthly, the most clinching indicator is that bank credit expansion on a year-on-year basis is currently over 32 per cent. A 30 per cent credit expansion has continued for over two years. The incremental credit-deposit ratio is well over 100 per cent and the average ratio is 71 per cent, which is clearly unsustainable. The asset base of banks has been built up by resort to non-deposit resources equivalent to 13 per cent of deposits. This is unsustainable. A pertinent question is, does an 8 per cent growth of the economy call for a 30 per cent credit expansion? A powerful viewpoint is that nothing should be done to hurt the growth prospects of the economy. Overextension of credit by banks would eventually result in a credit collapse and hurt real growth even more than an orderly deceleration of credit. When credit expands at very high rates there is misuse of credit as also misdirection of credit. Thus, the art of good credit management is a gentle deceleration of credit expansion.

Given this scenario, what sort of monetary and credit policy should be formulated? The essence of monetary policy is timely action. There is a need for a cautionary monetary policy which would bring about a gradual deceleration of the credit expansion. There should not be any sledgehammer measures, but equally there should be no measures which would open up the floodgates of created money via refinancing and reserve requirement reductions.

Thus, the only choice is a gentle signal for small incremental changes in interest rates. In the absence of clear signals from the RBI the credit expansion will continue unabated and as banks run out of funds there will be uncontrolled and chaotic increases in interest rates. The choices are clear.

Divya Bhaskar—March 20, 2006.

3 RBI Monetary Policy

A Fine Balance

The Reserve Bank of India Governor, Dr. Y.V. Reddy set out the Mid-Term Review on Monetary Policy on October 31, 2006. There was considerable media hype as to whether the Governor would go in for an overkill. The policy statement projects overall real growth at 8.0 per cent while retaining the forecast of inflation at 5.0-5.5 per cent. Both these projections could well be exceeded. Dr. Reddy has given thought about conflicting objectives but produced a policy which gives the right signals. The Governor did not do anything to hurt sustainable growth while not giving up his concerns about inflation. He has warned banks that they should live within their means and that if they knocked on the doors of the RBI they would have to pay a higher price. The media dissected every word in the comprehensive 70 page statement and the Governor has come up trumps: What a fine balance!

On the monetary policy front there is only one measure on the Liquidity Adjustment Facility (LAF) on which there has been considerable debate in the media and bankers. The debate is technical but depositors and borrowers need to understand what this is all about.

Under the LAF, the RBI announces a reverse repo rate i.e., the rate at which the RBI absorbs liquidity and a repo rate i.e., the rate at which the RBI injects liquidity in the system. These two rates set a corridor within which other short-term rates fluctuate, although there are times when certain short-term rates do go out of the corridor.

In the recent period, while the RBI was absorbing liquidity the reverse repo rate was the policy rate. When there is impending shortage of liquidity, the repo rate becomes the policy signalling rate.

From April 2005, the market was clued onto the reverse repo rate and the upward movement of the reverse repo rate was taken as a signal by banks to up deposit and lending rates. In actual fact, what the reverse repo rate signals is a rate below which other rates in the system should not fall.

During the last year and a half the reverse repo rate increases resulted in increases, albeit with some lags, in deposit and lending rates.

The increase in the repo rate from 7.00 per cent to 7.25 per cent, while retaining the reverse repo rate at 6.00 per cent, baffled a number of bankers. The increase in the repo rate while keeping the reverse repo rate unchanged is a clear signal that banks are being put on notice that they would have to pay more if they approach the RBI window for funds. It is curious that at a Round Table Conference of top bankers on November 1, 2006 the majority view was that interest rates in the system were unlikely to rise. With due respect to the experienced bankers it would appear that the bankers have misread the RBI signal.

Credit is rising at a fast clip of 30 per cent per annum while deposit growth is only 21 per cent per annum. It is obvious that sooner, rather than later, banks will run out of lendable resources. To use Dr. Reddy's phrase, the banks will have to rebalance their deposit and credit portfolios. While Dr. Reddy has conceded that the credit increase could be above the 20 per cent expansion indicated in April 2006, if credit expansion continues to increase at a rate of 30 per cent per annum, it would give the RBI some discomfort as banks would be knocking on the RBI doors for very large liquidity support. Thus, the message to banks is loud and clear that they should ensure that their lending is in consonance with their deposits. Since there are clear signs of liquidity shortages as the year progresses, the first off the block in gently raising interest rates on deposits and credit would be the bank which would be able to protect its bottom line.

Although the RBI has retained its projection for the inflation rate in 2006-07 at 5.0-5.5 per cent, the signs are that inflation could be much higher, possibly around 7.0 per cent. This is bad news for the *aam aadmi* especially as items which account for a large proportion of the consumption basket of the *aam aadmi* (e.g., wheat and pulses) show a significantly sharper increase than the overall inflation rate index.

Divya Bhaskar—November 13, 2006.

4 Timeliness Essential in Monetary Policy

The Reserve Bank of India (RBI) undertakes four quarterly reviews of monetary policy in a fiscal year—April, July, October and January. In a rapidly changing situation, RBI cannot remain content with predictable dates for monetary policy action. In April 2006, the RBI did not take any specific monetary policy measures though it did caution that there may be a need for policy action. In the event, the RBI raised the policy intervention interest rate by 0.25 per cent in June 2006. The June 2006 measure evoked disproportionate criticism partly because the RBI policy action was taken without a single line of explanation.

While undertaking, in October 2006, a mild 0.25 per cent increase in the repo rate (i.e., the rate at which the RBI injects liquidity), the RBI did caution that if the situation warrants, further monetary policy action would be undertaken. Furthermore, the top management of the RBI kept on reiterating the possible need for further measures.

In a brilliantly executed policy action on December 8, 2006, the RBI announced a monetary policy measure which market participants were not prepared for. The RBI raised the cash reserve ratio (CRR) by 0.5 per cent from 5.0 per cent to 5.5 per cent. Now, what is the CRR? The CRR is the instrument through which the RBI impounds excess liquidity in the system. In the Indian context, this instrument is the most powerful monetary policy instrument, especially as the RBI does not pay any interest on the impounded cash balances. Under the December 8, 2006 measure Rs. 13,500 crore will be impounded.

Why did the RBI undertake this measure at the present time? The RBI Press Release of December 8, 2006 provides cogent reasons for the policy action: (i) Real GDP growth in the first half of 2006-07 was 9.1 per cent, well over the full year estimate indicated in October 2006 of 8.0 per cent. (ii) The increase in non-food credit, up to November 2006, on a year-on-year basis, was 30.1 per cent as against 31.1 per cent a year ago. At this scorching pace of credit expansion, the banks will soon run out of lendable resources, resulting in a sudden disruption of credit flows with adverse impact on the real sectors. (iii) The money supply (M3) expansion, year-on-year, up to November 2006 was 19.4 per cent as against 17.3 per cent a year ago which is clearly too high. (iv) To mop up the excess liquidity, the government is bearing a heavy burden under the Market Stabilisation Scheme (MSS)—the balances increased from Rs. 29,000 crore at the end of March 2006 to Rs. 39,233 crore by the end of November 2006. With the CRR increase, the burden sharing is reasonably well distributed between government (MSS), RBI (Liquidity Adjustment Facility) and the banks (CR). (v) Although the wholesale price index (WPI) shows a year-on-year increase at the end of November 2006 of 5.3 per cent, as against 4.5 per cent a year ago, the consumer price index (CPI) up to October 2006, for various categories (industrial workers, urban non-manual, agricultural labour and rural labour) range between 7.2-8.4 per cent as against 3.2-4.6 per cent a year ago. The CPI, though lagged, gives a more accurate picture of inflationary pressures. (vi) More importantly, there are growing strains on domestic capacity utilisation which give clear signs of overheating of the economy. Overheating of the economy is a concept for which there is a total aversion in India as it hurts our macho spirits. Contrast this with China, a model many economists admire. The Chinese have, for quite some time, recognised the need to slow down the economy.

The art of good monetary management is to contain inflationary expectations and this is best done on the uptrend of the growth cycle. In other words, monetary policy measures have to be so timed that the economy creeps along the ceiling for growth as long as possible. In this context, the RBI has to be a party pooper when there are signs of the economy growing at a rate above its potential. If the RBI remains inactive it may be popular but failing in its duty of preventing the merriment of the party getting out of hand, resulting in a sharp downturn of the growth rate. Some observers have been critical of the RBI for spoiling the growth party and preventing predatory animal spirits from plundering the spoils while the bulk of the population groans under the pressure of inflation. Public policy cannot, and should not, be governed by the interests of a few predators and the RBI should not hesitate to take policy actions which are not approved by predators.

In the run up to the monetary policy review of January 30, 2007 what should be the policy stance? Too much should not be read into the October 2006 dip in industrial output. The economy continues to be overheated, inflation is still hugging the upper end of the comfort zone, non-food credit continues on a run-away expansion and there are no signs of a slowdown in capital inflows. In this context the RBI would do well to take pre-emptive action to reverse inflationary expectations. The RBI should, therefore:

(a) Raise the CRR from 5.5 per cent to 6.0 per cent, the phasing to be completed in February 2006, well before the March bank balance sheet window dressing. Paying interest on CRR balances is one of the sins of central banking. It is meaningless to impound cash balances and then give them back by way of interest. The lessons of the 1980s must be remembered, as interest payments rendered the CRR instrument totally impotent. The RBI should not be apprehensive of the capricious behaviour of the stock market fluctuations with screaming media headlines that the 'stock market has a CRR chill'. Stock market fluctuations can be attributed to almost anything!

(b) The repo rate should be raised from 7.25 per cent to 7.75 per cent i.e., a 0.50 percentage point increase instead of the usual 0.25 percentage point increase as time is soon running out for RBI action. The RBI should, to the extent possible, refrain from monetary tightening once it is clear that the downturn of the output cycle has started.

Divya Bhaskar—December 25, 2006.

5 Monetary Policy Initiatives and Banks' Response

The Reserve Bank of India (RBI) presented its Third Quarterly Review of the Annual Statement on Monetary Policy for the year 2006-07 on January 31, 2007. The RBI, for quite sometime, has been sending out cautionary signals. Rather than strong surgical intervention, the RBI has been resorting to mild homeopathic measures in the hope that the financial system is now mature enough to pick up the signals and undertake corrective action. But the banking system has, by and large, ignored the repeated cautionary signals and continues the credit binge. Banks have been partying blatantly to excesses as if there is no tomorrow. To have continued the reckless credit expansion, despite unequivocal warnings by the RBI, reflects sheer irresponsibility on the part of banks.

The RBI policy statement of January 31, 2007 is a veritable *tour de force* setting out, in no uncertain terms, the danger of continuing the current pace of credit expansion of 30 per cent per annum. This document will, in an historical context, become a *locus classicus* on the subject.

The RBI emphasised that there are continuing signs of aggregate demand firming up. The strong pick up in investment intentions, corporate business optimism, high growth of consumer durables and the high demand for credit from 2004, are all signals confirming the fears about overheating of the economy. In India, any reference to overheating raises heckles as this is considered as an affront to our macho spirits. The RBI, while recognising the increase in savings and investment, has concerns about the policy challenge of managing the transition to a higher growth rate while containing inflationary expectations so that the economy is on an enduring growth path.

The RBI is rightly preoccupied with containing inflationary expectation. Recognising the lags in the monetary policy transmission process, the RBI has been gradually withdrawing monetary accommodation since the middle of 2003.

It is now amply clear that the overall growth of the economy in 2006-07 is turning out higher than earlier envisaged (latest CSO estimates put it at 9.2 per cent). Inflation has risen to 6.58 per cent for the week ended January 27, 2007, outside the tolerable range of 5.0-5.5 per cent. Furthermore, the consumer price index reflects an even higher rate of inflation. Basic consumption items like wheat, pulses, onions and edible oils have shown disconcerting price increases.

It is to the credit of Governor Y.V. Reddy that in the January 31, 2007 Statement, he has unequivocally put overriding priority on fighting inflation. He argues that high growth benefits the poor with a lag while the impact of higher prices is immediate and, therefore, he emphasises that containing inflation is not only an economic necessity but also a moral compulsion.

Recognising the need for using multiple indicators and multiple instruments, the RBI has put emphasis on selective use of prudential measures, particularly in sectors which are showing clear signs of overheating such as real estate, outstanding credit card receivables, loans and advances reflecting capital market exposure and personal loans.

As part of monetary measures, the RBI has raised the repo rate (i.e., the rate at which it injects money into the system) from 7.25 per cent to 7.50 per cent. The Statement gives fair warning that unless the present excesses are not corrected quickly, harsher measures would be on the way and the RBI would use all policy measures, including the cash reserve ratio. The banking system has an incremental credit-deposit ratio which is clearly unsustainable. Access to the RBI window for funds has to be for very transient mismatches and use of RBI resources should not be for on-lending.

While some critics have argued that the bark of the RBI is frightening while its bite is innocuous, let not the banks say that they have not been warned. As such no measure by the RBI in the ensuing period should evoke squealing by the banks—they have been warned well in advance on more than one occasion.

On February 13, 2007, the RBI announced an increase in the CRR from 5.5 per cent to 6.0 per cent. The first stage of the increase comes into effect on Saturday, February 17, 2007; no doubt some banks who are not prepared for this measure would protest that insufficient time has been given to banks to adjust to the CRR hike. These banks should, in future, take the RBI's policy announcements more seriously. The January 31, 2007 review gave ample notice that a CRR hike was imminent. The absorption of Rs. 14,000 crore was of paramount urgency as part of inflation fighting and the RBI cannot be faulted. Some observers would consider this to be the end of the tightening. But we need to seriously consider whether the repo rate of 7.50 per cent is sufficient. We need to realise that given the deposit and lending rates of banks the repo rate is far too low. So long as the repo rate is well below the deposit rate and the prime lending rate is way above the repo rate there would be standing invitation to try and borrow from the RBI as much as the RBI would allow. This will require rationing. It is far better for the structure of interest rates *viz.*, deposit, lending and repo rate to be so aligned that there is a market clearing. Looked at this way, the present repo rate is woefully low. The RBI has taken a statesmanlike measure and not attempted to look for irresponsible popularity.

Divya Bhaskar—February 19, 2007.

6 Inflation

Dancing with the Devil

In India we deny the ravages of inflation so long as it is in the 5 per cent per annum range and everyone speaks in unison that inflation is a vice once it is in the 5-10 per cent range. Once inflation reaches double digits all howl for stringent measures. There is, however, little support when the central bank tries to take preventive action to prevent inflation from rising while it is still around 5 per cent. On a defensive note, the government innocently argues that inflation is only 6 per cent and that, after all, the fall out of such a rate of inflation should not be considered to be too detrimental to the interests of the *aam aadmi*. The expansionists deny that there is overheating of the economy and caution that control of inflation should not be at the cost of higher growth. The expansionists fail to realise that this is like trying to make an omelette without breaking an egg.

An unfortunate aspect is that there is considerable intellectual antipathy to quick, strong and effective monetary policy measures to control inflation. If one takes a random poll of leading economists stationed in Delhi (both within and outside the government) would one find an economist who would argue for unconditional control of inflation? Most of these economists would argue that real growth should not be sacrificed while controlling inflation. These venerated economists forget the basic dictum that growth can be achieved with rising prices, falling prices and constant prices.

The choice an economy makes relates to which price scenario to adopt, which in turn determines the distribution of income. Obviously, rising prices hurts the lower income groups the most. Thus, the choice is not between inflation and growth but inflation and the distribution of income.

The world over, price indices understate the true rate of inflation. In India, this is accentuated particularly as the policy triggering rate is the wholesale price index (WPI) which is available on a weekly basis with a short lag, rather than the consumer price index (CPI) which is available only on a monthly basis with a lag of two months and moreover, there are four CPIs depending on the segment of the population covered. In the recent period, some of the CPI indices show inflation edging close to the dangerous double digit level. True there is an element of transparency in India and there is no danger of a blatant fudge (e.g., in Argentina some items were just dropped from the CPI as these items showed explosive price increases).

Do the WPI and the CPI have any credibility in India? The answer of the *aam aadmi* is an unequivocal "No" as he is afflicted by intolerable price increases in a number of items in his consumption basket, such as wheat, pulses, onions, edible oils and milk; in the case of some of these items the increase is as high as 25 per cent over the year. Thus, the *aam aadmi* is skeptical about the official indices.

The *aam aadmi* is advised to invest his puny savings in safe fixed interest assets. Let us not delude ourselves that the inflation rate is 6 per cent—the true rate is probably close to 10 per cent. At a 10 per cent inflation rate a saver's asset of Rs. 100 is worth in real terms only Rs. 40 after 10 years. No wonder, senior citizens live in penury. Inflation is the number one enemy of the public and it is the moral responsibility of the monetary fiscal authorities to control inflation.

The RBI's tolerable level of inflation of 5.0-5.5 per cent appears too permissive. First, inflation tolerance, the world over, is coming down. Secondly, large tracts of the Indian population have no defences against inflation. Thirdly, the WPI has glaring deficiencies as an index of inflation.

In this context, the RBI needs to give single-minded attention to inflation control. If the government is serious about inflation, it should opt for a medium-term inflation mandate for the RBI. Our resolve to slay inflation should not be weakened merely because we are not sure which index to use, whether to track headline inflation (i.e., the overall inflation rate) or core inflation (e.g., excluding food and fuel) and how the medium-term is to be defined (e.g., three years or five years). We should not become prisoners of such flimsy excuses.

As the sage economist Professor P.R. Brahmananda said, "Not caring about inflation is like going into battle without caring for the wounded, the dying and the dead." Tolerating inflation is like dancing with the devil and those who argue against strong monetary measure to control inflation are the sinners of society.

Divya Bhaskar—March 19, 2007.

7 RBI Must Assault Inflation

The monetary policy of the Reserve Bank of India (RBI), is to be announced on April 24, 2007. After a prolonged period of policy dissonance, there appears to be broad consensus that the monetary policy has to be wielded firmly to deal with inflation. It is recognised that there could be overheating of the economy, in that the economy grows at an unsustainable rate, well beyond its potential and with capacity constraints the economy can face a sharp deceleration. Some key policymakers in Delhi are now talking about overheating, albeit in muted tones. It is pertinent to note that China—a country we all like to refer to—is openly talking about overheating and it is clearly directing policy instruments towards lowering the 9-10 per cent growth rate to about 8 per cent.

While the wholesale price index (WPI) shows an inflation rate of about 6.5 per cent, the consumer price index (CPI) reflects a much higher rate and some of the CPI indices show an inflation rate of around 9 per cent.

When the RBI takes mild measures there are shrill noises that the RBI could be making the same mistakes as in 1994-1996. While the bogey of 1994-1996 is raised unfairly to attack the RBI, there is a refreshing and percipient analysis of the 1994-1996 monetary policy episode by Rajeev Malik of JP Morgan Chase Bank (*Economic Times*, March 19, 2007). Rajeev Malik argues that there are no dangers of a replay of the 1990s boom-bust episode as India's current growth upturn has more solid foundations than the initial post-reform spurt in the early 1990s. He argues that the RBI is unfairly and incorrectly attacked for causing the downturn in the growth rate in the 1990s. He explains that in 1994, the RBI tightened monetary policy in the context of large capital inflows and once inflation decelerated by end 1995, RBI eased liquidity. He explains that Indian corporates overinvested in the early 1990s despite their inability to compete in the more liberalised environment. The GDP growth rate actually picked up following the monetary tightening of 1994 and the growth rate slumped only after 1996. Rajeev Malik argues that the current phase of monetary tightening by the RBI will moderate and not suffocate growth. Unlike in the early 1990s, the current industrial growth is broad based. Critics of the RBI would do well to imbibe Rajeev Malik's seminal article.

It is now increasingly accepted that the 9 per cent growth rate of the previous two years cannot be sustained in 2007-08 unless the structural bottlenecks in the infrastructure are eased and here the gestation lag is long. Nonetheless, it would be reasonable to expect a real growth of 8.0-8.5 per cent in 2007-08 as agriculture is expected to perform distinctly better in 2007-08 while the growth momentum in industry and service is still strong. The Union Budget is based on the premise that nominal GDP growth would be around 13 per cent and implicitly inflation is put at 5 per cent.

The latest year-on-year expansion of monetary expansion (M3) is 22 per cent that has the potential of an acceleration of inflation. If inflation is to be brought down on an enduring basis the M3 expansion should not be in excess of 16-17 per cent. Consistent with a deposit growth of 17-18 per cent, credit expansion should not be in excess of 20 per cent. This should be the backdrop against which the monetary policy for the first half of 2007-2008 should be framed.

The expansion of credit by 30 per cent in 2006-07 is unsustainable. The outstanding credit-deposit ratio on March 2, 2007 was over 74 per cent; this implies that banks have a large dependence on non-deposit resources. Furthermore, some large banks have a credit-deposit ratio as high as 88 per cent. At the scheduled March 15 tax payments, some banks were borrowing in the call money market at rates as high as 60 per cent (these rates are outliers and not average rates). Such banks which resort to reckless credit expansion deserve no sympathy and they are not exactly doing the country any service. The RBI should not take any measures to alleviate the problems of such banks.

The present monetary policy stance is accommodative and the RBI is behind the curve (i.e., the market is leading and not following the monetary policy). The present situation calls for decisive measures to curb inflation. The overall situation is admittedly complex with large capital flows and concerns about not letting the exchange rate appreciate to the point that it damages the economy. The RBI should aggressively use an admixture of a hike in the cash reserve ratio, the market stabilisation scheme (MSS) and a hike in the repo interest rate at which the RBI injects liquidity. Furthermore, the froth in capital flows needs to be moderated by suitable measures. All that the monetary measures would do is to crush inflation. There is no danger of an overkill and the RBI should act with resolution.

Divya Bhaskar—April 2, 2007.

8 RBI Speak

Its Finest Hour

The 84 page document by the Governor RBI, Dr. Y.V. Reddy on the Annual Policy Statement for the year 2007-08 dated April 24, 2007 is a collector's item. Analysts, columnists, practical bankers and other economic agents would always have something to crib about, but they all need to reflect carefully on the message that the document gives. Although the RBI has tried to progressively give clearer communication of policies and future outcomes, economic agents remain discontented. To put the present communication in proper perspective it is necessary to see it in historical perspective.

In the late 70s and the early 80s (essentially the I.G. Patel era), the RBI used cryptic and blunt language in communicating its measures. When there was monetary tightening, the RBI referred to the need to undertake a sharp credit squeeze and the entire communication on vital measures was undertaken in a short message. The RBI policy announcements got minimal attention—a half column or at best a column on an inside page. In the aftermath of the 1981-82 liquidity crunch, things changed drastically. The RBI was bitterly attacked in the media, by industry, bankers and the polity culminating in a Calling Attention Motion in the Rajya Sabha in which the then Finance Minister, Mr. Pranab Mukherjee, put up a brilliant defence of the RBI Governor; the proceedings of the debate should be mandatory reading for all economic agent who have an interest in monetary policy.

In the subsequent period, there was progressive elaboration of the rationale of monetary policy during the Manmohan Singh era (1982-1984) and the R.N. Malhotra era (1985-1990). During the Venkitaramanan era (1990-1992) there was a better recognition of why the RBI used harsh measures and the policies were appreciated as necessary in view of the precarious forex situation, and the RBI was somewhat more forthcoming in its explanation of policies.

The Rangarajan era (1992-1997) and the Jalan era (1997-2003) saw a progressive increase in communication to the market. In the Reddy era (2003-date) communication attained a pinnacle. It must be noted that both Dr. Rangarajan and Dr. Reddy had long stints as Deputy Governors' which no doubt contributed to the significant improvement in communication of policy. While the RBI and the government worked in perfect harmony during the 1994-1996 period, the government subsequently, totally disclaimed the RBI policy. As a result commentators to date, continue to launch ill-informed attacks on the RBI for the policies of the time. Even today, fears are expressed that the RBI can repeat the "so called mistakes of 1994-1996". Discerning independent analysts have, in the recent period, recognised that the RBI policies of 1994-1996 had nothing to do with the subsequent slowdown of GDP growth in the period starting in 1997-98 and subsequent years. The 1994-1996 period needs more serious analysis before commentators jump to the conclusion that the 1994-1996 policies were inappropriate.

In the recent era, post-2003, there has been a quantum jump in the detailed communication of policies. Yet, insensitive critics continue to attack the RBI communication policies. The October 2006 and January 2007 communications gave ample warning about the possibilities of monetary tightening in the subsequent months and economic agents caught napping have been critical that the RBI was not open enough and that the measures were an overkill.

The RBI had, months ago, cautioned about the problem of the overheating of the economy (i.e., the economy is running at a level which is not sustainable) and the dangers thereto. The RBI message was loud and clear but many agents who refused to absorb the lessons were subsequently discomforted when measures were taken in February and March 2007. If, at all, one can fault the RBI it would be that it was too explicit about what it would possibly do in the ensuing months. Central banking is not a precise natural science. The more the RBI elaborates policies, the more the critics take delight in criticising the RBI. It is by no means being implied that the RBI should clamp down on its communication policy. All that is suggested is that the RBI is already communicating all that is necessary and the RBI should not be egged on by the critics. The present macroeconomic situation is extremely complex and whatever the RBI does will be criticised by commentators. In an era when the media glare is 24×7 the RBI will be urged to reveal more and more information to an extent that the RBI would be urged to give, in advance, precise measure and their timing and it is obvious that the RBI just cannot do that.

The present communication skills of the RBI are excellent and the RBI should not be too concerned about the critics of its communication policy. It beholds commentators to understand that the RBI is today tackling an unprecedented complex situation and observers should try to understand what the RBI is doing rather than criticise the policy just to get some mileage out of criticism. Notwithstanding what the critics say, history will record the present situation as RBI's finest hour.

Divya Bhaskar—May 14, 2007.

9 Monetary Policy

Need for Further Tightening

In about three weeks, the Reserve Bank of India (RBI) would unfold its monetary policy quarterly review. What is the backdrop against which the monetary policy is to be formulated and what should be the ingredients of the policy?

The economy is growing at a pace much faster than envisaged a few months ago and the real GDP growth for 2007-08 will clearly be well over 9 per cent. The inflation rate as represented by the wholesale price index is around 4 per cent. Advocates of a faster rate of real growth would no doubt argue that with inflation down, it would be apposite to give a big push to a 10 per cent overall growth rate. The RBI would be well advised to keep in mind that there is still a strong possibility of overheating gathering momentum. The pressures on monetary expansion are likely to strengthen largely from the external sector.

Some argue that there are benefits from an appreciation of the rupee and hence, the authorities should not intervene in the forex market. While the costs of sterilisation are easily quantifiable, the damage to the economy of not sterilising capital inflows are much larger, though not easily quantifiable. What are the choices before the RBI? Quite frankly, there are no easy solutions. Some analysts advocate a "do nothing" policy. Taking note of the repercussions of policy actions, a broad framework for monetary policy is outlined.

First, the RBI should focus on the medium-term inflation rate and we cannot claim that we have already attained this objective.

Secondly, we should not get caught in the euphoria of a continuing appreciation of the rupee. On the contrary, we need to gradually claw back the real effective appreciation of the rupee.

Thirdly, preventing the real effective appreciation of the rupee would require more aggressive RBI intervention in the forex market and consequent sterilisation operations.

Fourthly, as a first step in moderating liquidity, the RBI needs to revamp the reverse repo facility under which the RBI absorbs liquidity at a fixed rate of 6 per cent on a daily basis up to Rs. 3,000 crore. The RBI must remove the lid of Rs. 3,000 crore or alternatively totally withdraw the reverse repo facility. If the facility is continued, there should be a variable reverse repo rate without a ceiling on the amount and the period of the repo should vary from 1 day to 28 days, depending on the RBI's perception of short-term liquidity. The RBI should be free to accept or reject bids.

Finally, the RBI should more aggressively issue bonds under the market stabilisation scheme (MSS).

Sixthly, the excess liquidity is bound to mount in the next three months and therefore, the cash reserve ratio (CRR) should be immediately raised from 6.5 per cent to 7 per cent. The RBI would no doubt be blamed for any adverse consequences if it were to directly raise the repo rate (i.e., the rate at which it injects liquidity) from 7.75 per cent to 8 per cent. The repo has become irrelevant as it is a sub-market rate and if a large demand for funds emanates from banks, RBI will be forced to ration injection of liquidity. On balance, the RBI should raise the repo rate.

How should the *aam aadmi* react to possible measures by the RBI? If there is a "do nothing" policy, depositors should immediately lock into one year or 590 days deposits offering the highest rate at the present time. If there is a CRR hike, banks are unlikely to lower deposit rates.

The savings bank rate of 3.5 per cent which is fixed by RBI is grossly unfair. When fixed deposit rates fell, the savings bank rate was, over time reduced from a peak of 6 per cent in 1992 to 3.5 per cent at present. Surely with the recent escalation of fixed deposit rates, it would only be appropriate if the savings bank deposit rate is raised. The argument against raising the savings bank rate is that these depositors use savings accounts as current accounts and depositors can always switch to short-term fixed deposits. This is an unfair, elitist view. There are large tracts of saving bank account holders who hold stable balances in semi-urban/rural areas and do not have rudimentary skills of investments. It is unconscionable not to raise the savings bank deposit rate. The savings bank facility is for small holders and individuals should not be allowed to have interest bearing savings accounts, in aggregate, above Rs. 1 lakh. It is not the task of the RBI to protect the upper income groups at the cost of the lower income groups. This is a serious issue and the RBI should not continue to be in a denial mode.

The RBI has an unenviable task. Whatever it does will be criticised, so it just as well should do what it deems appropriate.

Divya Bhaskar—July 9, 2007.

10 Monetary Policy Measures

Right Direction

What is attempted here is to set out in very simple terms the salient features and the measures. The simple version would no doubt lose the nuances which are replete in policy statements by almost all central banks the world over.

The RBI has persevered with its earlier projection of overall growth of the economy of 8.5 per cent for 2007-08. While, in earlier years, it made sense for the RBI to stick to conservative growth forecasts, continuing with conservative low projections carry with it certain hazards. In contrast, the Prime Minister's Economic Adivsory Council (EAC) has set out a projection of 9.0 per cent for growth in 2007-08. Given the somewhat better agricultural outlook and the continued strong growth in industry and services, there is a distinct possibility of the EAC's projection being exceeded. The downside risk could, conceivably, be that the RBI picks out the overheating of the economy somewhat belatedly.

The RBI, quite appropriately sets out its policy preference strongly in favour of price stability and the endeavour is to contain inflation close to 5.0 per cent in 2007-08 and 4.0-4.5 per cent over the medium term. The PM's EAC puts the inflation rate for 2007-08 at 4.0 per cent. While the RBI may have been weighed by the possibility of increase in crude oil prices, given that a number of countries are recognising the threat of inflation and emphasise the need to give policy signals of lower inflation rates being desirable, one would have hoped that the RBI would have been a bit stronger in pitching the inflation rate for 2007-08. One recognises that the finger would point at RBI if the projected inflation rate in 2007-08 is exceeded. It is in this context that the RBI may have opted to set out a slightly higher inflation rate in its policy statement.

Unlike in recent months, when liquidity management has been relatively less active, the RBI has clearly indicated that in the ensuing period it would use, more actively the cash reserve ratio (CRR), open market operations (OMO), market stabilisation scheme (MSS) and liquidity adjustment facility (LAF). Triggering all this is the appreciation of the rupee exchange rate which is now clearly hurting exports. In the absence of more vigorous forex purchases by the RBI the large capital flows would reflect in a further appreciation of the rupee. The large capital inflows have led to a massive increase in liquidity which, in turn, has lowered the inter-bank call money rate to as low as 0.1 per cent which is a standing invitation for misallocation and misuse of funds. The July 31 measures would, to some extent, restore call money rates to more normal levels.

What are the measures set out on July 31, 2007? First, the CRR has been raised from 6.5 per cent to 7.0 per cent from August 4, 2007: this will immediately reduce the excess liquidity by about Rs. 13,500 crore. Secondly, the ceiling of Rs. 3,000 crore on the amount the RBI absorbs under the reverse repo has been removed, and there are clear indications of variable interest rates and variable periods for the reverse repo. In other words, the reverse repo will be reactivated. Thirdly, the MSS would be used more aggressively.

What would be the impact of these measures? First, the RBI will have greater capacity to intervene in the forex market and at least stem any further appreciation of the rupee. Secondly, the RBI will have a better assessment of the actual excess liquidity through the reverse repo tenders. For the reverse repo to be effective it should be only a purely temporary parking slot pending a more enduring absorption of liquidity under the CRR and/or MSS.

The RBI faces an unprecedented complex monetary situation and has deftly taken the first step without disrupting the real sector of the economy. With continued capital inflows, the RBI will need to take further measures depending upon the emerging situation.

In the recent period, banks have been talking about reducing both deposit and lending rates. What should be the response of the *aam aadmi*? Depositors should encash on the present relatively high deposit rates. While deposit rates are unlikely to rise, they are also unlikely to fall in the ensuing period. Individual banks which try to cut deposit rates would only lose deposits to those who refrain from lowering rates. Lending rates would come down only if the government uses strong suasion to reduce interest rates; if banks reduce lending rates and are unable to reduce deposit rates their margins would come under pressure.

The RBI has used a fine balance to undertake a non-disruptive monetary tightening. To ensure that there is no resurgence in inflation, depending on the capital inflows, the RBI would need to stand ready to douse inflationary pressures by active monetary policy measures. All in all, the monetary policy measures undertaken on July 31 are in the right direction.

Divya Bhaskar—August 6, 2007.

11 Whither Monetary Policy?

Real gross domestic product (GDP) growth in 2007-08 is expected to be around 8.5-9.0 per cent, inflation is less than 4 per cent based on the wholesale price index (WPI), forex reserves have increased by about US$ 74 billion in the current financial year up to mid-December 2007, large capital flows continue, the stock market is booming and the rupee exchange rate has appreciated.

The broad money (M3) expansion on a year-on-year basis in early December 2007 is 21.4 per cent; what is more worrisome is the reserve money (created money) expansion of 32.5 per cent; as such monetary expansion in the ensuing period will be very strong. Deposit growth this year is 23.9 per cent while credit growth has admittedly been somewhat slower at 22.7 per cent. This portends a possible upsurge in inflation.

Developments in the industrial countries are a cause of worry. The sub-prime credit crisis in these countries appears to be more serious than perceived earlier and a number of large financial institutions are spilling out large losses. The central banks of these countries have reversed gears from inflation fears to concerns about recessionary trends and in response signalled ample liquidity and lower interest rates.

The pertinent question is what would be the impact on India. It is not clear whether capital inflows will continue to increase as investors in industrial countries seek higher profits or whether foreign investors will head back home to cover losses in their domestic markets.

Let us, for a moment, assume that more capital flows into India. In such circumstances what should the authorities do? To control excess liquidity the government is bearing a heavy cost through the market stabilisation scheme (MSS) bonds on which the government pays interest but does not use the resources; these bonds amount to Rs. 166,000 crore as of mid-December 2007 and the annual cost to government would be around Rs. 12,000 crore. The RBI has also raised the cash reserve ratio

(CRR) on banks from 4.5 per cent in March 2004 to 7.5 per cent at present; this implies an additional impoundment of the order of Rs. 90,000 crore.

Borrowers would no doubt put intense pressure on the RBI to reduce interest rates by signalling a reduction in the repo rate (the rate at which the RBI injects money). It could be persuasively argued that the inflation rate in India is low, interest rates in major industrial countries have been reduced and that there are fears that capital flows into India could slow down. To avoid a credit crunch to the "productive sectors", it could be argued that the CRR and the statutory liquidity ratio (SLR) should be reduced. Given the fears of an upsurge in inflation in the ensuing few months the RBI should not signal lower interest rates.

The RBI has to steadfastly avoid being persuaded by such seductive arguments. If capital inflows slow down or cease and net outflows are large, the RBI would need to rethink its strategy. It would be a serious error of policy if the CRR is reduced. Given the costs of sterilisation, the RBI should rebalance the sterilisation as between the MSS and the CRR. The additional impoundment under CRR is about Rs. 90,000 crore (at zero interest rate) while the MSS sterilisation is Rs. 166,000 crore (at about 7 per cent). If there is to be release of liquidity it would be best to reduce the MSS bonds to the point the additional impoundment since March 2004 (from the CRR hike) is equivalent to the outstanding MSS bonds. This way the average cost of sterilisation of excessive capital inflows would be 3.5 per cent or approximately what the RBI earns on its forex reserves. By using this balancing as its lodestar, the RBI can undertake large sterilisation operations without cost to the combined RBI and government accounts.

In the recent period, the RBI has been injecting sizeable amounts (up to Rs. 50,000 crore) via the reverse repo. Such injection has admittedly been erratic. If such injection becomes sustained it would be best to cut the injection and release a part of the MSS bonds.

If inflows increase substantially (the Institute of Economic Growth expects another US$ 25 billion to flow in by March 2008), the RBI should unhesitatingly impose a 10 per cent incremental CRR. The expansion of liquidity has swelled bank profits and as such the incremental CRR would only skim off the super normal profits of banks. It is only appropriate that there should be a fair burden sharing of the cost of sterilisation between the government, the RBI and banks.

The authorities should not countenance any appreciation of the rupee, in real effective exchange rate terms, but in fact should claw back a part of the appreciation of the past year.

While we feel that the sub-prime crisis in the industrial countries will not affect us, there are large non-performing assets in the Indian financial system which no one is keen to acknowledge. It would be a mistake to inject money into the system against the collateral of banks' loans.

Divya Bhaskar—January 14, 2008.

12 A Monetary Policy for All Seasons

The Reserve Bank of India (RBI) announced its monetary policy review on January 29, 2008. Characteristic of the RBI, the statement provides a comprehensive analysis of all aspects pertinent to monetary policy. To the hasty reader, the fact that the key policy signalling interest rates and the cash reserve ratio (CRR) have been kept unchanged tempts them to skip the rest of the masterly crafted document. But in doing so, the reader would be missing out on a treasure trove of knowledge on the ingredients of a policy decision.

The RBI projects GDP growth in 2007-08 at 8.5 per cent, somewhat below the 8.9 per cent estimated by the Prime Minister's Economic Advisory Council. While the expected growth in 2007-08 would be lower than last year, it would still be a historically high growth rate. The policy statement recognises that some segments of industry may be affected by the slowdown in demand, particularly exports, and therefore, there would be a need to keep a vigil on these segments.

The non-food credit expansion of scheduled commercial banks, on a year-on-year basis as of January 4, 2008, shows an increase of 22.2 per cent, which reflects a return to sanity after the frenetic increase of 31.9 per cent in the previous year. The deposit growth of 25.2 per cent, as against 22.9 per cent last year, points to the continuing large excess liquidity. What is of concern is that there is a sizeable increase in the costlier term deposits. The year-on-year monetary expansion (M3) of 22.4 per cent (20.8 per cent last year) is way above the desired trajectory of 17.0-17.5 per cent, which would, no doubt, be of concern to the RBI.

The question raised by some analysts is that if there is excess liquidity in the system, why has the RBI not lowered its signalling interest rates? Furthermore, these analysts point to the large reduction in the US Fed's interest rates. As the RBI policy document clearly brings out, there are a number of countries which have not lowered their signalling rates and moreover, some central banks have tightened interest rates in the recent period. Thus, each country has to take stock of its specific situation and formulate its own policies.

In contrast to the US, which is faced with the need to provide liquidity and lower rates to safeguard financial institutions hit by the sub-prime crisis as also the threat of a recession, India faces a situation of a continued high real rate of growth with the possibility of overheating of the economy, continued large capital inflows and all pointers are to a significant increase in the inflation rate. There are three points which need to be considered. First, the interest rate and inflation rate differentials cannot be considered exclusively in relation to the US; besides, the interest rates and inflation rates and the forward exchange rates are not properly aligned and as such one cannot take recourse to simple arithmetic. Secondly, it is not appropriate to compare the Indian wholesale price index with the consumer price indices in other countries. If the Indian consumer price index is used, the inflation differential between say India and the US would be higher. Thirdly, in India, there has been, for quite some time, an aberration of the RBI policy signalling rate being too low relative to deposit rates. The public sector banks' one year deposit rate is over 8.0 per cent while the benchmark base prime lending rate is 12.5-13.5 per cent. As compared with these rates the RBI repo (lending) rate of 7.75 per cent is clearly low (the effective cost of one year deposits is much higher taking into account the cash reserve requirements). The banks can always alter both deposit and lending rates without affecting their net interest margin, but this is a judgement call that banks have to take in the context of the excess liquidity which they park with the RBI at lower rates of interest via the reverse repo (wherein RBI absorbs liquidity).

The RBI has to balance domestic factors as also international developments. Given the lags in monetary policy, today's monetary policy has to take a view of the needs say 12-18 months hence. Given that capital inflows could be large or alternatively, there could be large capital outflows and the domestic real sector scenario and inflation rates could be very different, there is merit in the *status quo*. Far from such a policy being deficient, as some analysts would have us believe, the standstill policy would enable the authorities to deal with alternative scenarios. A point that many commentators seem to have missed is Governor Reddy's statement that the RBI would respond swiftly with both conventional and unconventional measures as deemed appropriate. The intent, content and actual implementation of policy could not have been set out in clearer terms. Governor Reddy and his colleagues need to be commended for delivering a policy for all seasons.

Divya Bhaskar—February 4, 2008.

13 Monetary Policy Stance

April 2008

The Reserve Bank of India (RBI) Annual Review of Monetary Policy is due to be announced at the end of April 2008. What should be the main elements of the stance of monetary policy?

The Union Budget for 2008-09 is clearly expansionary but under-funded which could unleash strong inflationary pressures in the ensuing period.

There is a considerable uncertainty as to the extent of capital inflows in the full year 2008-09 but in the immediate ensuing months, capital inflows are expected to continue to exert upward pressure on monetary expansion.

In recent months, a number of influential opinion-makers have been strongly advocating a softer monetary policy on the ground that inflation has been subdued. The underlying inflationary expectations, however, portend a pick up in inflation. Apart from the pressures of higher crude oil prices, international prices of food grains, particularly wheat, have risen sharply (India needs to undertake large imports of wheat in the ensuing few months). Metal prices are red hot which would put pressure on prices of manufactures. The latest figures for the wholesale price index (WPI) show a year-on-year increase of 5.91 per cent and there is sudden concern that the inflation rate is above the RBI's comfort zone of 5 per cent. The RBI monetary policy stance should not be determined by the week-to-week price movements but rather by the anticipated inflation rate over the medium-term. The medium-term outlook for inflation is clearly one of strong upward pressures. Moreover, the price indices understate the actual inflation rate and, therefore, the threat of inflation has to be at the top of the monetary policy concerns. The Prime Minister, Dr. Manmohan Singh, has decisively pronounced that inflation is the number one enemy of the public and if it is unchecked it could cause serious and widespread social discontent. Thus, as between a choice at the margin of a higher growth rate and higher inflation and a slightly lower growth rate and a lower inflation rate, the obvious choice should be for the latter.

Some segments in the industrial sector have witnessed a slowing down in recent months. This is to be expected given the frenetic pace of growth during the past 12-18 months. Now what is the outlook for the overall real growth of the economy in 2008-09? The Chairman of the Prime Minister's Economic Advisory Council, Dr. C. Rangarajan, has projected GDP growth in 2008-09 at 8.5 per cent. The Deputy Chairman of the Planning Commission, Dr. Montek Singh Ahluwalia, has projected a growth rate of 8.0-8.5 per cent. The Centre for Monitoring the Indian Economy has projected the growth rate at 9.1 per cent. These estimates contrast with the extremely gloomy estimate of J.P. Morgan of as low as 7.0 per cent. Given a modest growth of 10 per cent in services, 8 per cent growth in industry and a normal monsoon providing for a 3 per cent growth for agriculture, the overall growth rate in 2008-09 could easily be in the region of 8.0-8.5 per cent and this could be the backdrop against which the stance of monetary policy could be framed.

The real effective exchange rate (REER) shows an appreciation of 14 per cent. In recent months, the RBI has done a splendid job of preventing any further appreciation. An appreciation of the rupee is not in consonance with the fundamentals of the economy; a loss of 20 lakh jobs attributable to the appreciation just cannot be tolerated in a country like India. In 2008-09, the RBI should use every opportunity to aggressively claw back the REER appreciation of the rupee. It is a dangerous doctrine to try and control inflation by appreciating the rupee as the fall out is lower employment loss of competitiveness and lower output.

Despite its best efforts RBI has not been able to keep monetary expansion (M3) in 2007-08 within the desired range of 17.0-17.5 per cent. Critics of the RBI have accused it of following "monetarist" policies. It is indeed surprising that otherwise competent economists in India confuse "monetarism" with a cautionary monetary policy. Surely, the current annual rate of M3 increase of 22 per cent does not qualify for the distinction of a monetarist policy. Even the desired trajectory of 17.0-17.5 per cent would not be acceptable to the monetarist viewpoint which would call for a 12-13 per cent M3 expansion.

The overall stance for 2008-09 calls for a cautionary monetary policy and the RBI would do well to once again try to keep M3 expansion within a 17.0-17.5 per cent range. Such a monetary expansion would in no way hinder growth but would help moderate inflationary pressures. The RBI should be unmoved by the vitriolic attacks of the critics and it should persevere with an unswerving anti-inflationary policy. As Montague Norman, the longest serving Governor of the Bank of England said, "Dogs may bark but the caravan moves on".

Divya Bhaskar—March 31, 2008.

14 Monetary Policy Measures

April 2008

It is the fate of the Reserve Bank of India's (RBI) top management that it has to plough a lonely furrow. No wonder, 25 years ago, Prime Minister, Dr. Manmohan Singh called the Governorship of the RBI the loneliest job in India.

While there is always media hype about the April Annual Policy announcement, there is unusual interest this year as the wholesale price index has reached a 30 month peak of 7 per cent. Not so long ago, observers felt that inflation was benign; the focus was on growth and there was a clamour for softer rates of interest. With the spurt in inflation in recent weeks, public opinion has veered to the need for urgent measures. The fact is that the "true" rate of inflation is probably twice the official figure of 7 per cent and the *aam aadmi's* wrath is on the authorities. The supply side *wallas* are working overtime to put a ban here, a threat there and advocate a return to the pre-1991 type of controls. The supply side lobby does not see inflation as a generalised monetary phenomenon and debunks the view that monetary tightening is the need of the hour.

The RBI recognises that its job is to break the inflationary expectations and that monetary policy has a lag of 12-18 months. If at all, one has to criticise the RBI that it has not been harsh enough and fast enough in taking action to tighten monetary policy. The RBI should keep its sights on quickly dousing inflationary expectations; at present, it has a small window of opportunity to take strong monetary policy action. It is nobody's case that the RBI should go in for extremely harsh measures. At the same time, the RBI is not in the game of garnering populist applause. The job of the high priests in the temple of money is to undertake measures which may be unpopular but are the need of the hour to bring down inflationary expectations. Whether the measures are taken on or before April 29, 2008 (the scheduled announcement date) does not really matter. What should be the ingredients of the monetary policy measures?

Hike in the Cash Reserve Ratio (CRR): A hike in the CRR is a must for the April 2008 policy. The RBI should not wait for an avalanche of capital inflows before taking policy action. Rather than imposing an average CRR increase of say 0.5 per cent on outstanding liabilities, the RBI should, here and now, impose a 10 per cent incremental CRR. Thus, if the bank liabilities increase is large, a larger amount would be impounded and if the capital inflows are moderate less would be impounded. The incremental CRR, in a sense, puts the monetary policy machine on an auto-pilot and thereby eases policy tensions.

Hike in the Repo Rate: The repo rate i.e., the rate at which the RBI lends money to the banks, should be raised from 7.75 per cent to 8.25 per cent either in one step or two quick steps, but the sooner the better. The present reverse repo rate i.e., the rate at which the RBI absorbs funds from banks should be lowered from 6.0 per cent to 5.5 per cent for overnight money and the reverse repo rate for 14 days could remain at 6.0 per cent. These measures would widen the corridor between the repo and reverse repo rates but, as Governor Y.V. Reddy said, "widening the money market corridor is the price to be paid for uncertainty."

Lending to Individuals: In recent years the banks have gone berserk in increasing lending to housing, personal loans and the capital market. It was felt that lending to these sectors was totally safe. Mr. M.G. Bhide, the banking doyen, who now is closely involved with credit counselling, has for some time been warning, based on grassroots information that this is precisely the sectors where banks are going to face massive defaults. The bloodbath has to be allowed to take place and the RBI should stay away from a rescue operation. The RBI needs to give an unequivocal warning signal. What is more is that this is just the start, and large defaults in small scale and medium industry are likely. Thus, the banking scenario is indeed gloomy, notwithstanding the ridiculously high valuations signalled by the stock market.

Selective Credit Controls: There are advocates for a return to selective credit controls on individual commodities. The Indian experience from the 1950s to 1996 was that these controls just do not work. The RBI should not resort to tokenism.

The April 2008 policy is probably the toughest one the RBI has faced in over a decade. The RBI should refrain from populist policies which may please but damage the economy. As Tony Blair said: "The art of leadership is saying no, not saying yes. It is very easy to say yes."

Divya Bhaskar—April 14, 2008.

15 Central Bankers are like Firemen

The Reserve Bank of India (RBI) has been cautioning, for the past two years, about the dangers of inflation gathering momentum. The proponents of growth argue that the RBI is a spoilsport disrupting the merrymaking. The growthwallas dismiss inflation as a mere supply side matter in which monetary policy has no role to play. When the inflation rate touched 7.5 per cent, there was sudden commotion and the RBI was expected to use its magic wand to immediately douse inflation. The official inflation numbers are grossly understated and the common man's perception is that the "true" inflation rate is twice the official index. With years of excessive monetary expansion, is it a surprise that inflation has hit us? The life of RBI's top management is like that of firemen who are only required to risk their lives putting out raging fires caused by imprudent actions on which the RBI has given ample warning.

Now what is the message of Governor Reddy's April 29, 2008 policy announcement? The RBI perception is that GDP growth in 2008-09 would be around 8.0-8.5 per cent which puts paid to the bogey of monetary policy resulting in a sharp downturn. The RBI GDP projection is very realistic and monetary policy will not adversely affect growth. The RBI is of the view that the present inflation rate of 7.5 per cent should be brought down by the end of the financial year to 5.5 per cent. But there is a rider to the RBI projections on inflation *viz.*, monetary expansion (M3) should be brought down from the 20-21 per cent range to 16.5-17.0 per cent and this implies the need for further measures.

Advocates of a soft monetary policy argue that little or no further measures are required to bring inflation down to 5.5 per cent in 2008-09. International commodity prices have flared up and in India there is severe repression of inflation as the pass-through of crude oil and other prices has not been allowed. Moreover, with the large capital inflows (notwithstanding the recent slowdown in inflows) has generated large domestic liquidity. It is increasingly clear that we now have generalised inflation and not sectoral inflation relating to a few commodities. Furthermore, the fisc in 2008-09 is going to be very expansionary with the loan waiver, the Pay Commission Award and the political economy imperatives for large social sector expenditures. In such a situation, bringing down the inflation rate is going to be a Herculean task which will require monetary policy to put up the shutters.

The deft announcement of a 0.5 percentage point increase in the cash reserve ratio (CRR) on April 17, 2008 and the 0.25 percentage point increase announced on April 29, 2008 would immobilise about Rs. 27,500 crore. Proponents of a soft monetary policy argue that these measures would suffice and the RBI should just sit back and monitor the situation. Proponents of this approach are vehemently against the RBI raising its signalling interest repo rates (for lending) and reverse repo (for absorption of liquidity). There is a logical flaw in this approach. Curtailing liquidity through CRR hikes inevitably results in interest rate increases. Since public sector banks have been sternly warned not to raise lending rates, these banks are glibly talking about reducing deposit rates. This is a sure way to disaster. Banks would be well advised not to reduce deposit rates.

Monetary policy must be forward looking as it is effective only with a lag of 12-18 months. As such, it is imperative that the RBI has monetary control and that it does not react passively only after large liquidity sloshes around.

In the current financial year if there is further use of the average CRR, there would be policy tensions of repeated measures. Instead the RBI should very quickly impose a 10 per cent incremental CRR which would put monetary policy on an automat. If there is a need to inject liquidity, the market stabilisation bonds could be allowed to run off and the average CRR could be reduced. This way RBI would have monetary control.

My assessment is that during 2008-09 the RBI would be forced to raise its policy interest rates. By effecting early increases in interest rates it can avoid large hikes later which would shock the system.

The year 2008-09 is a watershed in monetary policy. If it tightens monetary policy it is damned. If it follows a popular soft monetary policy it would be damned by history for allowing inflation to devastate the economy. It is better that RBI face the wrath today than be condemned by history.

Divya Bhaskar—May 12, 2008.

16 Is Monetary Policy Too Tight?

The long delayed hike in the petrol price has triggered fears that the wholesale price index (WPI), with all its deficiencies of grossly understating inflation, would rise to double digit numbers.

Believers who worship growth over inflation argue that monetary policy should not spoil the growth story. On June 11, 2008, the RBI, quite appropriately, raised the repo rate (the rate at which the RBI injects money into the system) by 0.25 percentage point to 8.0 per cent. While the RBI has been concerned about inflation for quite some time, commentators see a gear shift in RBI's monetary tightening as the 0.25 percentage point repo rate increase comes 15 months after the previous increase in March 2007. Critics of the RBI argue that faced with excess liquidity in the system it is in order to raise the cash reserve ratio (CRR) but it should desist from raising the RBI's policy rate signal. There is the pious hope that when the RBI tightens via the CRR, interest rates would not rise. In response to the CRR hike, the normal response of banks would be to push up interest rates. But political economy considerations predominate as the government overtly advises banks not to raise interest rates. The facile solution is that banks should offset the decrease in margins by reducing deposit rates, conveniently forgetting that this action would further aggravate the tight funds position of banks.

Advocates of an accommodating monetary policy argue that the repo rate hike of 0.25 percentage point on June 11, 2008 would tighten money and affect the growth story. Despite the powerful clout of the lobby against monetary tightening, the RBI has sensibly followed an incrementalist policy while deploying its policy tools while dealing with an inflation situation far above the RBI's comfort zone of 5.0-5.5 per cent. Advocates of a loose monetary policy would perhaps concede that the June 11, 2008 repo rate increase of 0.25 per cent was inevitable but they would certainly not want the RBI to continue on the path of repo rate hikes.

The RBI has got itself trapped in very small repo rate increases. It may sound uncharitable to say that the RBI is aping industrial country central bank practices of very gentle repo rate increases. This is clearly flawed as the monetary transmission mechanism through the financial markets in India is extremely weak and this is precisely why strong interest rate action by the RBI is the appropriate policy response. It is argued that policymakers in the 1970s and 1980s were insensitive to markets, unlike today's policymakers and hence sharp increases in interest rates and cash reserve ratios would be inappropriate.

The upshot of all this is that the RBI is way behind the curve i.e., the policy responses are far below the market expectations. Reflecting this, markets have shrugged off all the RBI measures of the past two years. To effectively break inflation expectations, far more stringent measures are required. The French have a saying that you cannot make an omelette without breaking an egg. The problem in India precisely is that what we want is results without appropriate action. Given the present unacceptable inflation and political economy consideration which warrant that inflation be crushed quickly, say within the next six months, there is no option but to undertake harsh monetary policy measures.

Given the so called market sensitivity, the RBI would, in all probability, continue with small increment measures. If the objective is to get inflation down quickly, the choice is between a single sledgehammer approach of tightening which would shock markets and a series of rapid fire incremental measures.

While advocates of a soft monetary policy would groan that the CRR is already at 8.25 per cent, we need to recognise that China has a 17.5 per cent CRR. If capital inflows resume, there may be a need for a 2 percentage point increase in the CRR. The window of opportunity of policy action would be short and the RBI should gear up to quick 0.5 percentage point increases in the CRR.

On the repo rate, the RBI needs to move away from the 0.25 percentage point hikes to doses of 0.50 percentage point hikes. The need is for a repo rate close to 10 per cent. Advocates of a soft monetary policy would make shrill noises against such increases but to be effective the repo rate has to be somewhere between the one year deposit rate and the prime lending rate.

How does one finesse these measures? So long as the banks come to the repo window, the repo rate should be edged up. When banks come to the reverse repo window to park funds (i.e., when RBI absorbs liquidity) the CRR should be raised. Thus, the RBI has to undertake a flurry of policy measures to smoother the inflation monster.

To sum up the response to the question whether monetary policy is tight enough to deal with the emerging situation, the answer is that further tightening is warranted.

Divya Bhaskar—June 23, 2008.

17 Monetary Policy Tightening

The Need of the Hour

On June 24, 2008, the Reserve Bank of India (RBI) announced tightening of monetary policy. The repo rate i.e., the rate at which RBI provides liquidity, was raised from 8.0 per cent to 8.5 per cent. The cash reserve ratio (CRR) was raised from 8.25 per cent to 8.75 per cent. The rationale for the measures was clearly set out in a cogent four page press release. The unacceptable inflationary pressures are deeply embedded in the system as the wholesale price index (WPI) excluding fuel and food was 10.33 per cent as against 6.33 per cent a year ago. The RBI rightly argues that "in view of the criticality of anchoring inflation expectations a continuous heightened vigil over ensuing monetary and macro economic developments is warranted to enable swift responses, with appropriate measures as necessary, consistent with the monetary policy stance."

Critics of the RBI are at two extremes. A few academic scholars argue that the RBI has got its targets and instruments totally wrong and that monetary policy is in disarray. It is argued that the RBI should have a single formal mandate *viz.*, an inflation target and the RBI should just forget the exchange rate and let the markets take the exchange rate to wherever it does. The RBI should exclusively use the interest rate policy signalling instrument and eschew from use of reserve requirements (CRR) or forex market intervention.

The monetary policy doves, who disregard the excessive monetary expansion, believe that inflation is a supply side problem and that monetary policy has no role to play. Monetary policy tightening would adversely affect the real growth of the economy. Let us assume that interest cost is 10 per cent of total cost of production in an industry. Thus, a 1 percentage point increase in interest rates affects the cost of production by 0.1 per cent. If interest rate increases have such an insignificant impact on production cost, the legitimate question is why bother about using monetary policy. As Governor Dr. Y.V. Reddy has stressed, time and again, the role of monetary policy is to turn around inflationary expectations. A strong unswerving monetary policy has a crucial role in altering inflationary expectations.

There are observers who argue that the recent monetary policy measures are disruptive as the RBI has used instruments both to increase the cost of money and to reduce the availability of liquidity in the system. In reality, the RBI has well calibrated the measures so that monetary policy works towards altering inflationary expectations without being disruptive.

The RBI has resorted to small homeopathic doses of medicine and, ineluctably, such measures will need to be used regularly at short intervals in the immediate ensuing period. This is unavoidable as the RBI is clearly against a sledgehammer approach.

The problem the RBI faces is that the window of opportunity for measures is rather limited because of political economy considerations and accordingly, the RBI will have to use every window of opportunity to tighten monetary policy.

In the immediate ensuing period a monetary policy review is scheduled for July 29, 2008. One viewpoint is that having taken some measures on June 24, 2008 it would be best to wait and assess the impact of these measures. The difficulty with this approach is that the RBI is already behind the curve and this approach would further delay the necessary adjustment.

The other viewpoint is that the policy dose of June 24, 2008 is mild and stronger measures are required to quickly bring down the inflationary expectations which are still way beyond the RBI comfort zone. The market has already anticipated some action on July 29, 2008 and a lack of action would be interpreted as a weakening of the RBI's resolve. More importantly, the RBI should use every window of opportunity to tighten monetary policy. A moderate tightening is unlikely to affect growth. The bogey of growth being affected by a tight monetary policy has to be exposed. What a tighter monetary policy would do is to prevent inflationary expectations from becoming deeply embedded in the system.

To sum up, on July 29, 2008 the RBI should undertake the following measures:

(i) The repo rate should be raised from 8.5 per cent to 9.0 per cent; even this higher rate would not be a penal rate.

(ii) The reverse repo facility should be abolished as it is inconsistent with the policy of not paying interest on CRR balances. If this structural policy adjustment is not deemed appropriate at this stage, the present reverse repo rate of 6.0 per cent should be unchanged.

(iii) The cash reserve ratio should be raised from 8.75 per cent to 9.25 per cent (this will impound Rs. 16,000 crore of liquidity). A preferable alternative would be a 10 per cent incremental CRR which would put monetary policy on auto-pilot.

It is clear that the RBI measures taken so far are not sufficient to deal with the worrisome inflationary situation. Monetary policy credibility warrants immediate and decisive action.

Divya Bhaskar—July 7, 2008.

18 Steering Monetary Policy Through Difficult Times

The July 29, 2008 Review by the Reserve Bank of India (RBI) Governor, Dr. Y.V. Reddy, presents a balanced and accurate assessment of the complex macroeconomic situation and provides a plausible scenario for how the rest of the current financial year could unfold.

The RBI expects a slightly lower GDP growth of 8.0 per cent as against the 8.0-8.5 per cent projected in April 2008. The RBI projection is cautious and not unduly optimistic. The sectoral distribution of GDP with the sheer weight of services ensures that GDP growth in 2008-09 would be around 8.0 per cent. Any lagged adverse effects would, if at all, be probably felt in 2009-10.

The monetary expansion (M3), on a year-on-year basis as of July 4, 2008 at 20.5 per cent is somewhat lower than the 21.8 per cent in the previous year but far above the desired trajectory of 17 per cent. The year-on-year deposit growth of 21.7 per cent, up to July 4, 2008, was clearly lower than the 24.6 per cent increase in the previous year; in contrast, non-food credit expansion this year has been running at 25.9 per cent, which is higher than in the previous year (24.6 per cent). Given the series of increases in the cash reserve ratio (CRR), the incremental non-food credit-deposit ratio of 82.4 per cent this year (as against 68.8 per cent last year) is clearly unsustainable. In consonance with the desired trajectory of M3 of 17 per cent and a projected deposit growth of 17.5 per cent, the RBI is right to stress the need to bring about a significant and enduring reduction in non-food credit expansion to 20 per cent. The move by the RBI to focus supervisory attention on banks with excessive credit-deposit ratios is quite apposite. If suasion does not work, the RBI could consider suitable penalties for excessive credit expansion (there is a clear precedence for such a measure). The Governor has warned that, if necessary, unconventional measures would be resorted to.

The RBI identifies the uncertainties and the pressure points in the ensuing period *viz.*, the expansionary fisc and the international propagation of inflation. While these are vital imponderables, monetary policy has to be so modulated that the central objective of bringing down the inflation rate to the desired level is attained. The RBI does well to recognise that inflation is deeply entrenched and the RBI's comfort zone of 5.0-5.5 per cent cannot be quickly attained. Bringing down the current inflation rate of 12 per cent to 7 per cent by the end of the financial year is no easy task particularly as the RBI perception is that the present inflation rate is unlikely to come down in the immediate ensuing months. If the present inflation rate of 12 per cent is not quickly reduced to single digits, the desired objective of a 7 per cent inflation rate by March 2009 would be that much harder to attain.

It is against this perspective that the RBI's measures of July 29, 2008 need to be assessed. The raising of the repo rate from 8.5 per cent to 9.0 per cent with immediate effect was clearly warranted. The RBI seems to recognise that the repo rate is low in relation to other interest rates in the system.

The increase in the CRR from 8.75 per cent to 9.0 per cent is also in the right direction, but what is intriguing is that it kicks in only from August 30, 2008. Given the tax payments on September 15, 2008, one wonders why the RBI has waited till August 30, 2008 to make the measure effective; a preferable alternative would have been to make this measure effective immediately. If necessary, the RBI can still advance the date for the CRR hike (there is precedence for advancing the phasing of the CRR increase).

Given the constellation of factors affecting inflation, my own preference would have been for harder and faster measures, but it is one thing to offer advice without executive responsibility and quite another to take decisions with executive responsibility. The imperative need to bring down inflation rapidly will necessitate further measures between now and the October 24, 2008 Review.

What should the *aam aadmi* (common person) do? Depositors would be well advised to keep their deposits at the shorter maturities, say up to one year, as we have not seen the end of interest rate increases. Banks in turn would do well to now offer more attractive rates for the 2 years and 3 years maturities as, in all probability, deposit rates would need to rise further in the ensuing months. It is all a matter of conjectural variation where depositors and banks would attempt to size each other up.

Given the hard political economy aspects of implementing measures and the present inflationary situation, the RBI seems to have opted for a series of well modulated measures. One only hopes that RBI will have the window of opportunity to take further measures before October 24, 2008.

Divya Bhaskar—August 4, 2008.

19 Meaning and Significance of Monetary Policy for the *Aam Aadmi*

The Governor of the Reserve Bank of India (RBI), Dr. Y.V. Reddy, unveiled the third quarter review of the Annual Monetary Policy for 2005-06 on January 24, 2006. Prior to the announcement, the financial media predictions and analysis turned out to be directionless. About two weeks before the announcement, there were erudite write ups regarding the need for the RBI to signal an interest rate increase. But as the time came closer to the announcement, there were thundering headlines and editorials that a rate of interest increase would be unwarranted and that any signal of an increase in interest rates would have adverse effects on the growth of economy. In the event the RBI Governor, on January 24, 2006, did announce an increase in RBI's signalling interest rate. The issue for consideration is that does the monetary policy have any meaning and significance for the *aam aadmi* and if so, the relevance of these measures.

The measures announced were two-fold: (i) The fixed reverse repo rate was increased by 0.25 percentage point from 5.25 per cent to 5.50 per cent. In simple terms this means that RBI would now pay banks 5.50 per cent on short-term funds placed with the RBI under the Liquidity Adjustment Facility (LAF). (ii) The fixed repo rate was raised by 0.25 percentage point from 6.25 per cent to 6.50 per cent. What this means is that the RBI would now charge banks 6.50 per cent while lending to banks under the LAF. These measures relate to transactions between banks and the RBI. In the very nature of the RBI signal, banks could conceivably consider what they should do on their deposit/lending rates as also the pace of credit expansion.

Well before the RBI January 24, 2006 announcement, banks had been raising deposit and lending rates. It is a moot point whether banks were undertaking delayed responses to the October 2005 signals or were anticipating the January 2006 increases in interest rates by the RBI. Markets sometimes follow the RBI and sometimes lead the RBI.

Now what does all this hold for the *aam aadmi*? We should expect some increase in deposit/lending rates but the increases would be in the range of 0.25-0.50 per cent. The *aam aadmi* should not be lured into placing long-term deposits as interest rates are still on the upturn. As regarding bank lending the *aam aadmi* does not have much to fear about the increase in lending rates; they need to be concerned more about the availability of credit. There is a very large fringe of unsatisfied borrowers who have no choice but to go to the informal market where there are horrendous anecdotes of desperate borrowers taking loans at interest rates as high as 60 per cent per annum. In the context of the informal market interest rates, it is clear that there is no link between the formal and informal markets. The Rajamannar Committee, as part of the Banking Commission set up prior to nationalisation envisaged evolving links. While after bank nationalisation, these ideas were tossed out, the RBI and the government should take a relook at the Rajamannar Report which suggested suitable legislative changes.

There are possibilities of the economy overheating and it is only appropriate that interest rate increases are put through as the economy is on the uptrend of growth. In this sense, I think that the RBI's step was a good pre-emptive measure. Bloomberg, the internationally well respected wire agency, has put forth the argument that the raising of the RBI real growth of the economy estimate in the latest numbers is an admission by the RBI that the RBI interest rate hikes are not working (*DNA,* January 26, 2006). A correct interpretation would be that the RBI is perhaps the first agency, official or otherwise, to recognise that the growth for 2005-06 could be as high as 8.0 per cent. As the economy overheats, inflationary consequences are inevitable. Thus, the RBI's interest rate policy action should be seen as a step to control inflationary expectations.

The central issue of concern to the *aam aadmi* is inflation control. The Prime Minister, Dr. Manmohan Singh, many years ago, said that there can be no better anti-poverty programme than the control of inflation. The Finance Minister, Mr. P. Chidambaram, also many years ago, called inflation control the *dharma* of the RBI. Thus, the inflation preoccupation is in line with this thinking. The Bloomberg report referred to above, says

Governor Reddy's task is so onerous that the US Fed Chief's job seems like a breeze.

To sum up, the RBI's January 24, 2006 policy is tailored to the interests of the *aam aadmi*.

Divya Bhaskar—February 6, 2006.

20 Monetary Policy and Everyday Life

The Governor of the Reserve Bank of India, Dr. Y.V. Reddy, on June 8, 2006 announced a 0.25 percentage point increase in the reverse repo rate to 5.75 per cent (i.e., the rate at which RBI absorbs liquidity) and the repo rate to 6.75 per cent (i.e., the rate at which it injects liquidity). To the common person this may appear incomprehensible. The media highlights the measure in screaming headlines. The measure nonetheless does have relevance for the everyday life of the common person and it is necessary to understand, in simple language, what this is all about.

When the RBI raises or lowers its signalling rate, banks invariably, albeit with a lag, react by raising or lowering their lending and deposit rates and this is what is relevant to the common person.

Some years ago the interest policy changes by the RBI were few and far between and the changes were of the order of 1-2 percentage points on each occasion. But with the development of financial markets RBI no longer finds it feasible or desirable to make large increases in one shot. In the more recent period, the RBI's changes in interest rates have been of the order of 0.25 percentage point.

There are a number of reasons why the RBI signalled an increase in interest rates on June 8, 2006.

First, the RBI is concerned not only about the current inflation rate but expectations about future inflation rates. Dr. C. Rangarajan, Chairman of the Prime Minister's Economic Advisory Council, recently said that the petroleum price increase could add one percentage point to the overall price increase. Other commodity prices are also on the uptrend.

Secondly, the appropriate time for increasing interest rates is when the economy is close to reaching the peak of output. There are real sector cycles in output and if interest rate increases are delayed and effected when the economy is on the downtrend of the cycle, interest rate increases have adverse effects on output.

Thirdly, in the recent period, a large number of countries have raised their interest rates because of the threat of inflation. We, in India, cannot afford to ignore this international phenomenon as there would be large outflows of capital from India. There would be, after some time, higher inflation and this will force interest rates even higher. Thus, it is prudent to be in step with international interest rates. While interest rates in the United States are not the only factor, we need to note that the US Fed rate is an international pace setter. It is likely that the US Fed will raise its rate to 5.25 per cent at the end of June 2006. The present Indian policy rate is 5.75 per cent and the differential in interest rates is narrowing.

Now how should the common person react? A silver lining is that deposit rates are slowly going up. A depositor would be well advised not to lock in to very long-term deposits. It would be prudent to keep one's savings in one year fixed deposits while interest rates are on the uptrend. Actually, small savers would be well advised to keep a portion of their savings in the nine per cent Senior Citizens Scheme of the Post Office (this can be also done through banks) and a part in Monthly Income Schemes of Mutual Funds which invariably yield returns well above that on bank deposits and moreover, the income is tax free. Admittedly most bank depositors prefer to hold some fixed deposits with banks on precautionary considerations. The late M.R. Pai said that banks live off the ignorance of depositors. When small depositors wake up, banks will get a rude shock as those who invest in bank fixed deposits will exodus from banks. In short, the deposit interest rate structure of banks is low and unsustainable.

As for small borrowers, they would be well advised to quickly lock themselves into fixed interest rates on their loans for purposes such as housing, education and other personal loans. This is advisable as we have yet to see the end of the upward movement of interest rates.

There will no doubt be frenzied write ups in the media as to whether Governor Reddy would raise RBI's signalling rate on July 25, 2006. Any erudite forecast would be a wild guess. The common person should plan his or her decision on a cautious assumption and therefore, protect himself/herself from increases in interest rates. Given the sagacious approach of the

RBI, it would take all factors into account while deciding on interest rate changes and the parameters could well change between now and July 25, 2006. The RBI decision is probably the best kept secret as the RBI's top management itself may not make up its mind till the last minute—that's the art of central banking!

Divya Bhaskar, Monday, June 26, 2006.

21 RBI Monetary Policy Review

The Reserve Bank of India (RBI) Governor, Dr. Y.V. Reddy, set out the monetary policy review on July 25, 2006. This is a technically superb document which spells out in detail the background against which certain policy measures were announced on July 25, 2006. There is, however, a need to pick out a few observations in the document to enable the reader to get some idea of what this is all about and the implications for the *aam aadmi*.

The RBI raised the reverse repo rate (i.e., the rate at which the RBI absorbs liquidity from banks) from 5.75 per cent to 6.00 per cent. Furthermore, the repo rate (i.e., the rate at which the RBI injects liquidity into the system) was raised from 6.75 per cent to 7.00 per cent.

Now why did the RBI raise these interest rates? There are a number of reasons but for our purpose a few of these reasons can be listed and explained in lay language. While simplifying these issues we would no doubt miss some of the nuances but, hopefully, this would not materially affect the *aam aadmi*'s understanding of the central issues.

First, the overall stance of policy is to ensure an environment under which the growth of the economy can continue while maintaining price stability; here there are concerns that inflation could go out of hand and, therefore, pre-emptive measures need to be taken to counter any acceleration in inflation. Secondly, a number of countries have increased interest rates and in this context India also had to increase interest rates. Thirdly, taking into account various developments, including the increase in international oil price and the increase in other commodity prices, maintaining the inflation rate within the desired range of 5.0-5.5 per cent called for policy action. Fourthly, the credit expansion in 2006-2007 so far is running way above the desired trajectory of a 20 per cent annual expansion. Taking all these developments into account the RBI was justified in stepping up its signalling rates by 0.25 percentage point.

The question on everyone's mind is whether this is the end of the interest rate increases or would there be further increases in the remaining months of 2006-07. My own assessment is that there would be no let up in the international oil price and there is a strong possibility of interest rates rising further in at least some countries. In the domestic economy, with a continuing strong growth of the economy, the explosive increase in credit would continue. The danger of such a scenario is that the banks will just run out of lendable resources and sooner or later there would be a disruption in credit flows to the productive sectors. The RBI would certainly not want such a scenario to emerge and therefore, further hikes in interest rates appear unavoidable in the remaining part of 2006-07.

How do the RBI signalling rates impact on other interest rates in the system? The RBI rates impact on deposit and lending rates of banks. My assessment is that a series of interest rate increases would be required during the remaining part of 2006-07 to contain credit expansion within the desired range. It is conceivable that mere interest rate increases would not be enough and other measures would be necessary to reduce liquidity in the economy. In the absence of further measures the ugly head of inflation would resurge, warranting even harsher measures.

What should the *aam aadmi* do? Depositors should be wary of falling in the trap of the 5-year deposit now being canvassed by banks. There are reports that the 5-year deposit may be given the Section 80 C benefit. Depositors have to realise that by locking themselves in longer-term deposits they would be denying themselves the benefits of higher interest rates. Depositors would be well advised to restrict their deposit maturities to one year.

To the extent that one is a borrower, it would be best to lock into a fixed rate loan. The longer one delays the taking of a loan, the higher would be the rate. There could well be a stampede to obtain credit and in the melee, the small borrowers would be the ones to suffer.

The earlier the RBI takes action, the less the burden on the small depositor/borrower. Thus, one should welcome the RBI's interest rate signal of July 25, 2006.

Divya Bhaskar—August 7, 2006.

II

22 A Peep into Inflation and Interest Rates in 2006

The real rate of growth in 2005-06 is likely to be 8 per cent (government spokesmen coyly say it would be 7 per cent). Inflation on a year-on-year basis is below 5 per cent. In such a euphoric milieu, eminent economists tell us that inflation in 2006 would remain benign and interest rates should not be allowed to rise. The Ministry of Finance's view is that nothing should be done to disrupt growth. Industry likes low rates of interest and therefore, corporate sector interest rates should not be raised. If interest rates are to rise, the increases should be restricted to personal loans and real estate.

The world over, countries are undertaking monetary tightening. Indian interest rates cannot be immune to interest rate changes abroad. The European Central Bank, after almost five years, has increased interest rates. The US Federal Reserve Bank has recently continued its relentless increase in interest rates.

We must compliment the government and the Reserve Bank of India (RBI) for undertaking deft measures to prevent the large excess of liquidity from having an adverse impact. It is felt that this excess liquidity will work itself off and hence interest rate increases are unwarranted. What would happen if Indian interest rates do not increase while interest rates abroad rise? It is certain that capital will flow out of India and this will result in a sharp and disruptive increase in interest rates in India.

The simple arithmetic is as follows: the interest rate differentials between India and the United States should reflect the inflation rate differentials and the interest rate differentials between India and the US should reflect in the forward premium/discount on the exchange rate. If we do not take note of these fundamentals, there would be serious monetary instability.

Responding to the mild signal of monetary tightening in April 2005, Suman Berry, Director General of the National Council of Applied Economic Research (NCAER) argued that there are real costs associated with tightening too soon or too hard and the merrymaking should have been allowed to continue. Reacting to the very mild tightening in October 2005, the NCAER argues that the increase in interest rates cannot be properly justified.

Abheek Barua, Chief Economist, ABN Amro hopes that the RBI would not go in for interest rate hikes to contain demand. Subir Gokarn, Chief Economist, CRISIL is also clearly against monetary tightening.

In a recent article in *The Financial Express* (December 6, 2005), on 'Tracing Inflation', Christopher Lingle of the Centre for Civil Society, New Delhi presents a contrarian viewpoint. Lingle argues that although economic theory has disproved the notion that rising costs can push up overall prices, media commentators cling on to this misguided notion. There is only one source, namely artificially cheap credit engineered by loose monetary policy. It is pertinent to mention that Lingle is a Professor from Guatemala.

In India, during the last two years, the credit expansion has been 30 per cent per annum and the incremental credit-deposit ratio for the two years taken together has been over 100 per cent. If this pace of expansion continues for a further two years, the outstanding credit-deposit ratio will be over 75 per cent; and banks will default on statutory cash and securities requirements.

The benchmark prime lending rate (BPLR) of major banks is 10.25-10.75 per cent but 60 per cent of lending is at below BPLR. We now have an interest rate structure wherein banks lend at a wide range of interest rates (6.5 to 16 per cent). Term deposit rates of major banks range between 5.25 to 7 per cent. It is *hara-kiri* for banks to lend at rates below the maximum deposit rate. To avoid cut-throat competition, banks have recently tried to agree to a common floor lending rate but have been hit by cartelisation provisions of the Monopolies and Restrictive Trade Practices Commission (MRTPC).

What is likely to happen in 2006? Monetary policy will certainly be sensible. Banks will soon feel pressure on their liquidity and raise deposit rates marginally, say by 0.5 to 1 per cent. With the guidance from the Ministry of Finance, banks will be reluctant to raise rates for the corporate sector beyond an increase of 0.5 to 1 per cent. But borrowers in the personal segment should be prepared for sharp increases in interest rates.

With RBI's emphasis on price stability and ample availability of foreign exchange to undertake adequate supply management, the authorities should be able to contain inflation at 5-5.5 per cent. But if the authorities hesitate to take appropriate and timely action, inflation could well rise to the upper reaches of single digits.

Divya Bhaskar, Monday, December 26, 2005.

23 Interest Rates Have Nowhere To Go But Up

Recently, there has been considerable public debate about the seemingly different interest rate signals from government and the Reserve Bank of India (RBI) and there is a perception that banks are like a nut in a nut cracker. Quite apart from whether all this hype was necessary, the basic question remains as to what message the *aam aadmi* should glean from these developments. For any meaningful answer we must move away from the media hype and discuss the less exciting but more relevant issues. In this connection we need to note certain incontrovertible facts.

First, the Indian economy continues to show strong signs of growth of close to 8 per cent in 2006-07 and this is strengthened by the more recent favourable trends in the monsoon.

Secondly, while it is now well accepted that Indian interest rates have to take cognisance of international interest rates, too much could be made about the August 8, 2006 pause in the US Fed Rate after 17 successive 0.25 percentage point increases which amounts to a 4.25 percentage points increase over the past three years. During the same period Indian signalling rates have risen by only 1.5 percentage points. Thus, India has a lot of catching up to do. Interest rates are still rising in other industrial countries and even if the US Fed skips an increase at the end of September 2006, our interest rates would be hopelessly out of alignment with the rest of the world.

Thirdly, Indian money supply expansion, on a year-on-year basis, is running close to 20 per cent which is well above the desired trajectory of 15 per cent. It has been fashionable in recent years to downplay the relevance of money supply. The hard reality is that that ultimately excessive monetary expansion results in inflation and in this country, with large tracts of poverty, we cannot afford to take chances with inflation. As the late Professor P.R. Bharamananda said: "Not caring about inflation is, like going into battle without caring about the wounded, the dying and the dead."

Fourthly, the credit trends in 2005-06 were clearly worrisome with an unconscionable increase in credit of well over 30 per cent. In the current financial year the trends upto July 21, 2006 point to a credit expansion of well over twice the pace of last year; moreover, if we take cognisance of the fact that the March 31, 2006 base was highly distorted by the year-end window dressing on March 31, 2006, the credit increase in the current year is clearly unbridled.

Fifthly, the large short-term excess liquidity is not really short-term as it continues to persist over an extended period of time. To say the least, this is extremely dangerous as it is precisely under such circumstances that there is misallocation of credit and what is worse misuse of credit.

Sixthly, it is estimated that banks can finance out of deposits only a 20 per cent credit expansion in 2006-07. This implies that there will be a sudden cessation of credit as the banks run out of funds. This is clearly going to be disruptive.

Seventhly, the cheap money policy of recent years had resulted in 60 per cent of credit being disbursed at sub-prime lending rates. While this was a joy-ride for large borrowers it was certainly iniquitous for small borrowers.

The advocates of low interest rates argue that weaker sections are hurt by high interest rates, while the fact is just the opposite. The weaker sections are just not in a position to borrow. The weaker sections have a higher share in deposits than in credit.

The recent report of the Prime Minister's Economic Advisory Council, chaired by Dr. C. Rangarajan, has recently confirmed that some hardening of interest rates is necessary. All this implies that interest rates must and will go up in the next 12-18 months.

Now what does all this have to do with the *aam aadmi*? Whatever the inclination of the government and the RBI there is little that they can do about the unavoidable increase in interest rates. If the authorities adopt a benign policy of soft interest rates and accommodate this with created money, inflation will go out of hand and force interest rates up. If the authorities follow a proactive monetary policy before the situation goes out of hand, interest rates will rise. In simple terms, there is no alternative to higher interest rates.

The *aam aadmi* has nothing to fear. Depositors should patiently wait for higher interest rates and not be enticed into the five-year deposits; they should keep to the one-year maturity. If one is a borrower, please borrow quickly as a scramble will develop and small borrowers would be pushed aside.

Divya Bhaskar—August 21, 2006.

24 Post-Diwali Interest Rates

A Review of Monetary Policy of the Reserve Bank of India (RBI) is slated for the end of October 2006. What do the post-Diwali stars hold for the *aam aadmi*? It is surprising how strong the lobby is against interest rate increases. It is not for nothing that 25 years ago Dr. Manmohan Singh described the RBI Governor's post as the loneliest job in India.

Now what are the forces lined up against interest rate increases? First, the US Fed after 17 successive 0.25 percentage point increases took a pause in the last two reviews. It is argued that this is a signal for India to follow. If we do this, we would be ignoring the policy responses in other major economies. Secondly, it is argued that with robust real growth of the economy we need to stimulate investment and what better way than a pause in the interest rate hikes of the recent period; it is further argued that it will be ideal if we lower interest rates. Thirdly, inflation rates are currently benign and fractionally below 5 per cent. Fourthly, industry likes low interest rates. With all these factors, the low interest rate lobby is rooting against any further increase in interest rates.

There are, however, a number of strong reasons tilting towards a hike in interest rates.

First, with the current financial year continuing to show strong real growth there are signs of the actual real growth rate exceeding the potential. Unless the brakes are applied gently now, real growth may jerk up which would be unsustainable.

Secondly, the inflation rate does not fully reflect the increase in petroleum and other commodity prices. As the oil price pass through has not been complete, any reduction in the international oil price over the peak level is not sufficient justification for a roll-back in domestic petroleum prices.

Thirdly, monetary policy operates with a considerable lag and there is no let up in the expected medium-term inflation rate.

Fourthly, broad money (M3) is growing at an annuated rate of 20 per cent, way above the desired trajectory. Credit growth in the current financial year continues to be strong at an annuated rate of over 30 per cent. This is dangerous as there is misallocation and misuse of credit. There is a tendency to pat one's self for the reduction in non-performing assets (NPAs). As we enter the third year of a 30 per cent annuated credit increase in recent years has an increased weightage in the outstanding credit and this artificially brings down the percentage of NPAs. We need to be prepared for an increase in NPAs.

Fifthly, the RBI had earlier estimated that the banks resources would sustain only at 20 per cent credit expansion; while deposit growth has been higher than earlier projected, it just cannot sustain a credit growth of 30 per cent. If the present pace of credit expansion continues, banks will run out of resources in the second half of 2006-07 resulting in a cessation of credit with deleterious impact on output and employment.

Sixthly, the interest rate differentials between India and major industrial countries are too low and do not reflect the inflation rate differentials.

The Economic Advisory Council to the Prime Minister chaired by Dr. C. Rangarajan in its report (August 2006), has stated that some hardening of interest rates is inevitable to restrain inflation and that containing the expansion of money supply has to be an integral part of inflation management.

All this points to the need for India to continue its cycle of well calibrated interest rate increases. A pause in the interest rate increases at this point of time could well trigger off a sharp outflow of capital with obvious undesirable consequences. Thus, there is a strong case for at least a small increase in interest rates. It is argued that the increases in interest rates in the recent period have been inadequate. While this could be a case for sharper interest rate increases, it must be recognised that there is a considerable lag in the monetary policy transmission. Given that the earlier increases are yet to be fully transmitted, very sharp increases could be disruptive. It would, therefore, be desirable to persevere with small calibrated increases in the RBI signalling rate by 0.25 percentage point.

Now what should the *aam aadmi* do? The depositors should keep to the short end of the maturity structure as deposit rates are likely to rise in the January-March 2007 quarter. As regards borrowers, they should quickly lock into fixed interest rates. The *aam aadmi* need not fear interest rate increases as relatively lower income groups have a larger share in deposits than in credit. In short, rising interest rates are in the interest of the *aam aadmi*.

Divya Bhaskar—October 2, 2006.

III

25 Budget Curtain Raiser

We all have our fears and aspirations of what the Union Budget for 2006-07 will hold for us. It is increasingly being recognised that the manoeuvreability is limited with limits to taxation and rigidities in expenditure. Before discussing a few specific issues relevant to the budget, it would be useful to look at some of the macro perspectives.

The Central Statistical Office (CSO) has put the real rate of growth for 2005-06 at 8.1 per cent. Given that key fiscal ratios are measured in relation to the gross domestic product (GDP), the commitment on the gross fiscal deficit (GFD) for 2005-06 of 4.3 per cent for the Centre could be attained. This would boost the morale of those assigned to projecting the GFD for 2006-07 to argue that we are on track to attain the trajectory set out in the Fiscal Responsibility and Budget Management (FRBM) Act.

This has encouraged optimists to argue that with an unprecedented three-year average growth rate of 8 per cent, the Indian Elephant has overtaken the Asian Tigers and soon could well top the inter-country growth charts. It is well understood that the leaders of the country, who understand the intricacies of the growth process, are giving a clarion call of marching towards a 10 per cent growth rate for the ensuing few years, more as an aspiration rather than a serious forecast. The danger is that investment decision takers might be convinced by these aspirations and go in for over-investment (i.e., investments in excess of resources available) and therefore, an inflationary resurgence could be a strong possibility. It is hoped that somewhere along the line the key budget documents will provide the GFD and revenue deficit ratios with explicit assumptions for 2006-07 for real GDP growth and inflation.

A source of worry is that while recognising the imperative need to channel more resources to the infrastructure, a powerful viewpoint is emerging that, at the margin, there could be a trade-off between a larger GFD with higher allocations for infrastructure. Estimates are that an additional Rs. 100,000 crore per annum would be required for the next three years merely for railways, roads and ports. While there is some private investments in small ports, it is unlikely that there would be significant private investment into these sectors which have long gestation lags before the investments yield results. In the ensuing budget it is unlikely that there would be any significant taxation or reduced subsidies or reduction in other current expenditure. In other words there is, in all probability, not going to be any fundamental change in the Union Budget.

The Inter-Ministerial Committee chaired by Dr. C. Rangarajan has reportedly recommended that the LPG and kerosene subsidies should be phased out. The LPG subsidy per cylinder should be reduced by Rs. 75 now and the balance subsidy of Rs. 145 should be reduced by Rs. 25 per quarter. The kerosene subsidy of Rs. 12 per litre should initially be reduced by Rs. 1 per litre and the subsidy targeted only to specific target groups. The proposals of the Committee are eminently suitable but one needs to await the political economy of implementing the changes.

The stock market is booming and the rise in the recent period is spectacular. At some point of time investors would want to encash on their gains especially as long-term capital gains of over one year are totally exempt from income tax. Dr. Shankar Acharya, the eminent economist, has made a pre-eminently suitable proposal under which long-term capital tax should be raised from 0 to 10 per cent, short-term capital gains tax raised from 10 per cent to 20 per cent and the securities transaction tax reduced by one-half. The total removal of long-term capital gains tax was unconscionable and a redressal would be in order.

The 80 C deduction from income set out in the budget of February 2005 has not as yet been operationalised by February 2006. Morally the Government should just back-off. Public provident fund, retirement plans and insurance should be out of the EET—Exempt (investment) Exempt (interest) and Tax (withdrawal)—and the EET should be restricted to Equity Linked Saving Schemes. The whole EET scheme was ill-prepared and the Government has to pay the price of vacillation.

Bank deposits have become the most serious victim of the interest rate/tax regime of recent years. An 80L type concession exclusively for bank term deposits of over one year needs to be introduced.

The total exemption of dividends from companies and mutual funds is an atrocity in a just society but the plutocracy will use all its force to resist a tax on individuals on dividends from companies and mutual funds.

So what can the *aam aadmi* expect—he can only fear and pray.

Divya Bhaskar—February 20, 2006.

26 A Budget with Compassion

The Union Budget for 2006-07 does not exactly set the elite on fire. But in fairness, the budget does endeavour to meet the mandate. That the fruits of growth are shared with the masses, particularly the deprived, the dispossessed and the downtrodden. In this context, it is necessary to appreciate the various programmes—Bharat Nirman (essentially rural upliftment) and the flagship programmes relating to the North-eastern region, the Sarva Siksha Abhiyan (primary education), the Mid-Day Meal Scheme, Drinking Water and Sanitation, the National Rural Health Mission, the National Rural Employment Guarantee Scheme and other programmes to improve the standard of living of the weakest segments of society. All these are commendable efforts and must be persevered with. It is sad that when anything is done for the poor, it is called populist but when goodies are distributed to the elite they are labelled as productive use of resources.

The old age pensions granted under the National Social Assistance Programme to destitute persons above the age of 65 years at Rs. 75 per month is woefully inadequate and the Budget for 2006-07 raises it to Rs. 200 per month from the Centre and states are asked to supplement it by another Rs. 200 per month making a total of Rs. 400 per month for each person identified as a destitute. This is, perhaps the single most compassionate measure in the Budget. As happens to most deserving causes, the devil is in the detail. How does a social worker identify a destitute? Invariably the destitute has no fixed address and lives beyond the pale of both urban and rural society. This does not mean that we just give up. An alternative thought is to set up large number of shelters to provide basic *dal, roti, kapda* and minimal accommodation to the destitute; the able-bodied could be encouraged to participate in the work of these shelters.

The Budget provides for a direct interest subsidy of 2 percentage points on farm credit liability upto Rs. 100,000 per borrower. For 2006-07 short-term credit will be provided to farmers for a principal amount of Rs. 300,000 at a rate of interest of 7 per cent with a refinance subvention from NABARD. The extent of interest rate subvention and the proportion of refinance needs to be carefully calibrated to ensure that banks do not lose in the process. Purists would argue that the banking system should not be used as a vehicle for subventions.

The appointment of a Committee on Financial Inclusion is welcome. To reach out to the mass of cultivators beyond the pale of the formal and informal credit systems it is necessary to get rid of the obsession of killing the informal sector as also the unrealistic passion for low interest rates. The policymakers of today must study the Report of the Rajamannar Committee which was set up before the nationalisation of banks in 1969.

The measure to transform the recapitalisation bonds of banks to SLR bonds will create problems for the government borrowing programme and put an upward pressure on interest rates (something that the government does not want). This had best be shelved for the time being. The increase in the FII ceiling for investments in government paper will, at best, have a very marginal effect.

The increase in the ceiling on aggregate investment of mutual funds in overseas instruments from US$ 1 billion to US$ 2 billion is a long overdue measure. Furthermore, the removal of the 10 per cent reciprocal holding in a company in India is a salutary measure.

While the revenue deficit and the fiscal deficit are projected to come down in 2006-07 there is a fly in the ointment. The nominal GDP projection is not revealed and in the absence of transparency no assessment can be made on the extent of fiscal consolidation.

It is unfortunate that there is a lack of clarity on how the EET system will work under Section 80 C. The *aam aadmi* is at the mercy of rumours and or calculated leaks. There are vague references of a gradual introduction of the EET system and the operation of an "EET House". In the absence of any clarification the investor is left twirling in the wind. Till a clarification, investors would do well not to use the PPF as an instrument under 80 C as there could be punitive consequences. Again, investors should stay away from long-term deposits with banks for five years as interest rates are on the uptrend. One hopes that before the Finance Bill is passed the

Finance Minister will table an unequivocal statement in Parliament on the operation of EET system.

The overall assessment is that the budget addresses some major issues of distributive justice but operational and statistical problems mar an otherwise good budget.

Divya Bhaskar—March 6, 2006.

27 Light at the End of the EET Tunnel

In the Budget of February 2005, the Finance Minister, P. Chidambaram announced a major revamping of the concessions for income tax payers. The central feature was that the Section 88 tax rebate and the Section 80 L deduction from income were abolished and instead a deduction from income under Section 80 C upto Rs. one lakh was introduced. But there was an important rider. The extant EEE system (under which the investment was exempt, the income was exempt and the withdrawal was exempt) was to be replaced by an EET system (under which the investment was exempt, the income was exempt but the withdrawal would be added to income and taxed in the year of maturity/withdrawal).

When it came to operating the EET system, a host of irresolvable issues emerged. Illustratively, while provident funds were to be covered by the EET scheme and annual contributions would enjoy the Section 80 C deduction, on withdrawal/maturity the entire corpus would be added to income. This would be a cruel burden, especially for retirees. There is the knotty problem of segregating balances prior to the introduction of EET.

The government appointed a Committee chaired by Dr. R. Kannan, an economist-cum-actuary. The Kannan Committee Report has been submitted many months ago but is under wraps. Transiting from EEE to EET has not been easy to implement. Accordingly, the Budget of February 2006 was silent on EET except that bank deposits of over 5 years were added to the list of instruments eligible for the 80 C concession. In other words, the EET regime has not as yet been introduced.

It is indeed gratifying that after a great deal of confusion, there is light at the end of the EET tunnel. The government, as part of greater transparency, has announced that it would soon set out a Discussion Paper before implementing the EET system. This is a salutary measure which will enable a viable system to develop after an open debate.

First, although the EET system may be in force in certain countries, we need to recognise that in India pension plans cover only a minority of the population. In the case of pension plans it would only be appropriate to tax the annual pension. Surely it would not be intended to tax the corpus in the pension plans as the corpus does not accrue to the beneficiary who only receives the monthly/annual pension.

In India a relatively larger segment is covered by provident funds than pension plans. As provident funds are to be subject to EET the burden on retirees would be horrendous. Illustratively if a person contributes Rs. 70,000 per annum for 15 years, the corpus, at an 8 per cent rate of interest per annum would at the end of 15 years be Rs. 17 lakh. If this corpus is taxed at 33.6 per cent, the corpus would be reduced to Rs. 11.3 lakh. Thus, instead of earning Rs. 1,36,000 per annum on the corpus of Rs. 17 lakh, the individual would earn only Rs. 90,000. There is a pressing need to exclude both pension plans and provident funds from the EET system. If for some imperative reason provident funds are to be covered by the EET system there should be a clear choice for investors. All existing provident fund account holders should not be covered by the EET system and only accounts opened after a specified future date should be covered.

An enervating question would be as to what to do about the Section 80 C concession in the case of pension plans and provident fund accounts. For these two categories, the deduction could be only 50 per cent. The 100 per cent deduction should be only for instruments covered by EET.

Secondly, in the case of equity linked savings schemes (ELSS), the Section 80 C concession could remain at 100 per cent, but EET applied on the entire corpus on withdrawal/maturity. An advice to investors would be to always opt for dividend and pay out and not for the growth option.

Thirdly, the National Savings Certificate (cumulative option) has an inbuilt mechanism of annual interest being included as income and taxed; thus this scheme should be totally out of the Section 80 concession and therefore, not subjected to EET.

Fourthly, while banks have agitated and got the Section 80 C concession investors would be best advised to avoid the cumulative option. In the event this will neither help the depositor or the banks and is a non-starter.

Fifthly, the Section 80 C concession for housing and educational expenses is a misfit in the 80 C family.

To sum up, the transition from EEE to EET should be very gradual and some dilution would be desirable.

Divya Bhaskar—April 3, 2006.

28 Tax Returns for Non-Business Individuals

In the recent period there has been considerable turmoil on the issue of the forms for filing tax returns for non-business individuals. For these tax payers there is the 2D and 2E Forms and now the 2F Form. It is unfortunate that a well intended effort to streamline the tax return forms has hit into a storm.

The existing Forms 2D and 2E were, by themselves, reasonably simple though the forms did have some deficiencies. First the 2D Form, though a single large sheet was required to be filled in duplicate. Imagine the kind of gymnastics one has to undertake to fill the form. There is always the danger of inadvertent errors as one flips one side to fill the second side. Again, there was clearly inadequate space to fill details in certain columns. Moreover where there are alternatives such as resident/non-resident, the tax payer was required to strike out what was inapplicable; thereafter, the tax payer is provided space to fill in the appropriate items. Again, as one tries to read the instructions one needs to have a pilot's vision or use a magnifying glass. Furthermore, the tax payer is not required to provide a photocopy of the advance tax, self-assessment tax. The purport being that this clutters up papers in the income tax office and such information would be redundant as the tax authorities would have all tax deducted details as also information on self-assessment tax on their giant computers. The ground reality is that a large number of individual tax payers receive terrifying notices that they had wrongly filled in their PAN number and/or that while investing in debt instruments like Saving Bonds or the Senior Citizens Saving Scheme, the tax payers has not revealed the PAN number. On providing documentary evidence that the allegation is not correct the concerned tax officials shrug off the issue and do not follow it up. Now why does this happen? Tax payers who are to be provided refunds are to get their refunds before the end of the next financial year to which the return relates. To ensure no delay on the part of the tax authorities these letters are sent out to ensure compliance with the refund rules. Surely, in this day and age there should not be a resort to such opaque practices.

Turning to the much maligned 2F Form, let us look at the positive features. First, the form is not to be filled in duplicate and there is a single sheet acknowledgement form. Secondly, the instructions for the 2F Form do not need a pilot's vision. Thirdly, the 2F Form has enough space to fill in details without squeezing in the details in microscopic writing. Now the negative features. First, it is understood that the tax authorities do not want detailed back up papers to clutter up their offices. In the absence of the detailed back up provided by the tax payer, the tax authorities would end up asking endless questions. Secondly, the form up front puts in bold letters that TDS certificates, proof of payment of advance tax/self-assessment should not be enclosed. It would seem that the tax authorities would wish to move over to a 'trust based system'. The ground reality is the tax payer is now required to give details of the 'TDS circle where the Annual Return under Section 206 is to be delivered', the 'Tax Deduction Account of the deductor' and the date of payment/credit of the tax. The Forms 16 and 16A information provided sometimes run into two pages with details of credits to government account and here again the new form has no space to fill the details, while the details of Forms 16 and 16A as provided by the deductor cannot be attached. Thirdly, there is the problem of the cash flow statement. The tax payer, to meet the requirements, would need to have attachments which are prohibited and one would need the help of chartered accountants. Fourthly, there is no minimum cut off for income where the cash flow is required. Are we headed for a Kaldor type expenditure tax of the 1950s which was a total failure even though it was a brilliant idea in theory?

Surely, one can salvage the efforts of the tax authorities. In this context the following could be considered:

(i) The basic structure of Form 2F could be retained.

(ii) The TDS details should be allowed to be attached. Surely we cannot expect the tax payer to vouch for the tax deduction authority.

(iii) The cash flow statement could be dispensed with for gross incomes below say Rs. 10 lakh per annum.

(iv) The tax authorities should undertake random surveys of the realities at the grassroot levels by directly talking to a sample of individuals as to the problems they encounter.

Divya Bhaskar—July 26, 2006.

29 Fiscal Injustice at its Worst

One of the basic principles of public finance is the recognition that the fisc should undertake expenditures for the public good and that taxation should take into account the capacity to pay or in other words there should be distributive justice. In India we seem to pay lip service to these laudatory objectives. A closer look would, however, bring out that in India we have examples of the worst kind of fiscal injustice. What is more distressing is that the perpetration of such injustice is supported across party lines and successive governments have sanctified such atrocious policies.

There is abundant literature on fiscal privilege which results in certain segments of society getting unconscionable high rates of return because of the tax system. A common illustration of this was the tax free Relief and Savings Bonds. We cringe at giving poor bank depositors higher rates of interest but we do not object to high net worth individuals enjoying unlimited tax free incomes. In the aftermath of public discussion on these high rates of return, successive expert Committees by Dr. Y.V. Reddy, Dr. Vijay Kelkar and Dr. Partha Shome, resulted in the closure of tax free bonds.

Since 1997, yet another loophole has emerged in the form of dividends being tax free in the hands of the ultimate beneficiary. Supporters of the measure have argued the rationale of such exemptions with great skills. First, since the corporation pays tax, taxing dividends amounts to double taxation. Secondly, it is cumbersome to deduct tax at source and then follow up on tax payments by individual beneficiaries. Thirdly, there is a dividend distribution tax so there is no loss of income to the exchequer. Fourthly, with a booming stock market the benefits far outweigh the costs. Fifthly, dividend beneficiaries need to be encouraged as they take risks.

The issue of tax free dividends has been extensively debated and eminent economists have brought to the notice of the government that the system of a total exemption of dividend income without any limit is unconscionable. Since 1997, the dividend tax exemption has generated considerable policy turbulence. In the first stage, the dividend distribution tax was raised to 20 per cent and in the second stage it was lowered back to 10 per cent (plus surcharge). In the third stage, the dividend tax free status was withdrawn and the system reverted to the pre-1997 position. In the fourth stage, the dividend tax free status was restored.

The advocates of tax free dividends having drawn blood saw to it that dividends from mutual funds were also made tax free without any limit.

But that was not the end of greed. The entire tax system was sacrificed at the altar of the capital market and long-term capital gains on financial assets transacted on the stock exchanges were exempted from capital gains tax. As if all this was not enough, short-term capital gains tax was lowered to 10 per cent along with a token securities transaction tax and this too has been lowered for frequent traders.

In contrast to all these give always, small savers are now being massacred and threatened on their small savings such as the Senior Citizen Scheme. The move from an exempt (investment), exempt (income) and exempt (on maturity) i.e., the EEE system is being replaced by an exempt (investment) exempt (income) and tax (on maturity) i.e., the EET system. The Kannan Committee was to work out the modalities of how the system would work. To think of it the whole new system is a brutality. In this country there are vast tracts of the population without social security cover and these individuals attempt to put by small savings for their old age; one-third of their savings corpus would be sequestered. Why have not the detailed operation of the EET system been made public?

We are meant to be a just society but we practice the opposite. If we claim to be a government for the *aam aadmi*, the government should undertake a basic overhaul of the tax system. Surely, the government is not meant to be exclusively for the blatant self-interest of the plutocracy.

In this context, the following should be considered: (i) Dividends in the hands of the final beneficiary should be free from income tax only up to Rs. one lakh per annum. (ii) Long-term capital gains tax should be reintroduced on financial assets transacted on the stock exchanges. (iii) Short-term capital gains should be treated as any other income and taxed at normal rates. The capital market would not collapse because of a capital gains tax. In any case the tax system should not be a prisoner of the capital market. (iv) The EET system should not be applied to long-term superannunation schemes like public and other providend funds.

If we do not undertake such redressal of the fiscal atrocities of recent years, then it would only be proper to conclude that we support the segment of Greek philosophy which argues that "Justice is the interest of the stronger".

30 Fiscal Policy

Some Macro Perspectives

There are various targets set out under the Fiscal Responsibility and Budget Management Act (FRBM). A few months ago there were strong rumblings that the FRBM targets would be relaxed and it seemed as if the expansionists would win the day. It was felt that with the higher than expected growth and the need for expenditure to support the economic and social infrastructure, it would make good sense to deviate from rigid fiscal targets. Reputed economists felt that the FRBM targets were flawed. Fortunately, wiser counsels have prevailed and the FRBM targets have not been relaxed. To put it in Dr. Isher Ahluwalia's pithy words: "The FRBM is like a chastity belt, don't loosen it without a better alternative."

The FRBM targets provide for an annual reduction of 0.3 percentage point in the Centre's fiscal deficit and a 0.5 percentage point reduction in the revenue deficit. There is considerable euphoria that the fiscal targets for 2006-07 will better the targets. Now, it must be appreciated that the targets are set out as a percentage of GDP and as such, with buoyant GDP growth in 2006-07, well beyond the wildest expectations, the denominator would be larger and hence the targets will be comfortably attained.

While the performance on the fiscal front would be viewed as a proportion to GDP it is also useful to look at the numbers in terms of the absolute fiscal targets. As per the FRBM the revenue deficit in the first half of 2006-07 was not to exceed 45 per cent of the full year's deficit; the actual revenue deficit is over 80 per cent of the full year's projected absolute deficit. Again, the fiscal deficit in the first half of 2006-07 was 68 per cent of the full year's absolute target as against an indicated 45 per cent of the target. The fiscal expansionists would argue, not without force, that the targets are in GDP terms and not in absolute numbers. While conceding this argument it bears stressing that the FRBM targets would be met for 2006-07 because of the buoyancy of GDP growth. As we go through the inevitable cycle of GDP growth, the 2007-08 fiscal targets will be that much more difficult to achieve. Hence, there must not be excessive euphoria about the FRBM targets for 2006-07 in terms of GDP.

The strong GDP numbers have made some forecasters go overboard e.g., the firm Oxus. The combined fiscal deficit of the Centre and States is projected at 4.8 per cent of GDP in 2006-07. My own view is that such forecasts are wildly optimistic and should be totally discounted. For such optimistic forecasts to be achieved, there would be a need to undertake massive throw forward of expenditure from 2006-07 to 2007-08 and this could make the attainment of 2007-08 targets even more difficult to attain. The Finance Minister, Mr. P. Chidambaram, has a perfect record of each year's budget estimate of the Centre's fiscal deficit being lower than the previous year's deficit. I, for one, would go as far as to use the Gujarati phrase to say, "I would burn my moustache" if the combined deficit of the Centre and States in 2006-07 turns out to be as low as 4.8 per cent of GDP."

While there are strong reasons for being resolute about not deviating from the fiscal targets, it makes little sense to undertake a drastic fiscal compression in one year only to significantly relax the FRBM target the next year. The attainment of the revenue deficit target of zero deficit by 2008-09 is something worthwhile pursuing. Furthermore, the bulk of the revenue surplus should be earmarked for debt repayment—India has one of the highest debt GDP ratios and a serious effort should be made to bring about a significant and enduring reduction in this ratio. Internal debt is a silent killer and an internal debt explosion can be very sudden.

There is merit in moving over to a concept of public sector borrowing requirement (PSBR) to include the borrowing requirements of public sector bonds. The PSBR would be about 3 percentage points of GDP above the gross fiscal deficit. The PSBR is the true measure of the public sector deficit.

Divya Bhaskar—January 8, 2007.

31 Need for Clarity in Tax Treatment of Small Savings

For the past few years there has been considerable sabre rattling on withdrawal of tax concessions on savings. Section 80 L and Section 88 have been withdrawn and Section 80 C has been introduced.

Two years ago, the Finance Minister put savers on notice that there would be a move from an exempt (investment), exempt (income) and exempt (maturity amount) i.e., from an EEE system to an exempt (investment), exempt (income) and tax (maturity amount) i.e., an EET system. There was the Kannan Committee but little authentic information has been put in the public domain. Many questions remain unanswered. For instance, if one has a Public Provident Fund (PPF) which has run, say 12 years, would the entire amount at maturity be taxed after the 15th year? Despite a number of unanswered issues, the Section 80 C concession was formally introduced under which investors could claim exemption from income in the year of investment up to Rs. one lakh with the general proviso that the maturity proceeds would be added to income of the year of maturity.

There are calculated leaks that the government is likely to grant an exemption from the EET system for certain select instruments like providend funds, insurance and pension schemes up to 2010-11 and thereafter the EET system will be fully in force. In a 15-year PPF scheme there would be serious iniquities along the maturity structure. What has queered the pitch is that investors have taken credit under Section 80 C (up to Rs. one lakh) for Assessment Year 2006-07 and will do so for Assessment Year 2007-08.

In a country where social security does not exist for large tracts of the population, there is little merit in aping the industrial countries which have strong social security systems and follow the EET regime. We should be more sensitive to our situation and work out an appropriate indigenous solution.

First, EET should never be made retrospective as it would be violative of the terms under which the investments were made before the change over.

Secondly, the best course would be to totally exclude schemes like PPF and insurance/pension schemes from EET. For such schemes the investments should not be given any benefit in the year of investment but the income in each year and the maturity corpus should be free from tax. Of course after the maturity of the scheme the income accruing to the investor from investment of the corpus should be subject to tax.

Thirdly, EET should apply only to a few schemes like the Equity Linked Savings Schemes (ELSS) and bank deposits of a five-year maturity period.

Fourthly, transiting from a Section 80 L cum Section 88 regime to a Section 80 regime, with a heavy rear end tax, is messy and the authorities would be well advised to undertake a comprehensive review before finalising the change over.

Fifthly, there are strong pressures to bring back the 80 L deduction from income for bank deposits for five-year deposits, exempting income up to Rs. 15,000 per annum. It is best not to give ad hoc concessions. It is better to raise the general exemption level and not provide individual concessions.

Sixthly, instruments like PPF, insurance and pension schemes should not be covered by EET. In such cases the TEE system could be considered. In other words, these schemes should not be provided the 80 C deduction at the time of investment. Equally, the annual income and maturity proceeds should not be taxed. The income, once the corpus matures, would no doubt be subject to tax. The reason for not taxing the annual income on these schemes is that the income does not come into the hands of the saver. The time has come to cut through the morass of confusion and to set out a definitive operative schemes.

Seventhly, there is talk of introducing tax deduction at source on the Government of India 8 per cent taxable bonds. This would be in order, provided the threshold is sufficiently high. More importantly, the government has conveniently, forgotten that interest rates have risen substantially since 2003. Either the 8 per cent rate on this scheme should be raised or the scheme should be scrapped. The promised easy trading in government securities remains a mirage.

Finally, we talk so much about taxing the savings of small investors which hurts the vulnerable segments of society. Yet we do not have the stomach to bite the bullet on the large and unlimited dividend tax exemption which is a clear rip off. If the dividend tax exemption is to continue, it would be necessary to limit the tax exemption on company and mutual fund dividends to, say Rs. one lakh. To have a system of unlimited exemption of dividend income is grotesque. The argument that corporates are taxed and, therefore, dividend recipients should not be taxed is not sustainable. After all, it could be argued, that salary earners pay tax and, therefore, should not be required to pay any indirect taxes on the products they buy. If such logic is pursued, there would be no tax collection. The unlimited exemption from tax for dividends should be capped. Would anyone listen—not even the so called champions of the *aam aadmi*!

Divya Bhaskar—January 22, 2007.

32 A Caring Budget

The Union Budget has now become a *Maha Tamasha* evaluated by experts. In the instant polls the majority put their thumbs down on the Budget. Ideally we need to know the median gross (including tax free) income of these experts and those participating in the polls. The ostensible reason for the negative vote was because there were no major tax breaks for the top one per cent of the income pyramid. These poor folks at the top of the pyramid are afflicted by the enhanced education cess, enhanced dividend distribution tax and the extension of the minimum alternative tax. The increased outlays for the rural sector, education, health and social security schemes are criticised by the elite on the ground that they do not permeate to the intended beneficiaries. The real challenge is not to cut down these allocations but to ensure efficient distribution. It is only apposite that a caring government recognises the ravages of inflation.

The Budget cannot be faulted for emphasising inclusive growth, equity and social justice. The larger allocations for school education, particularly upper primary and secondary, means-cum-merit scholarships, Mid-day Meal Scheme, the *Aam Aadmi* Bima Yojana for death and disability insurance for rural landless households and health insurance for senior citizens are social objectives which cannot be ignored.

The Finance Minister has an enviable track record of adhering, year after year, to fiscal deficit targets. Of course, in the recent period, the targets have been met with the help of higher nominal GDP which is the denominator in the fiscal deficit targets.

India Incorporated and foreign investors would be disappointed that there are no exciting reform measures. But it bears reiterating that upliftment of those at the bottom of the pyramid is a prerequisite for enduring reforms and that is precisely what the present budget does.

There are two measures which need close examination. First the India Infrastructure Finance Company Limited (IIFCL) is to set up two subsidiaries abroad. The IIFCL will borrow forex from the RBI and the first subsidiary would use these funds to provide foreign exchange support to India infrastructure companies so as to leverage further borrowing abroad. The second subsidiary would use RBI forex reserves to invest these funds abroad, to earn higher returns than obtained by RBI at present, by investing in securities which the present RBI Act does not allow. Let us pause and think over the issue. The RBI has a 70-year record of managing the forex reserves and how is the fledgling IIFCL better able to handle forex reserves? I do not know why we do not do things the right way. A jumbo consortium of financial institutions and banks should raise the rupee resources and buy the forex from RBI. Alternatively, the government should provide the rupees to buy the forex. But we want to adhere to the FRBM so we run quasi-fiscal deficits with all sorts of contrived devices. The defence would be that Singapore, China and Botswana did this so why not us? To use forex reserves transparently the government should introduce legislation to set up two wholly owned subsidiaries of RBI which would have the statutory powers to do what is being done through the back door. It is the duty of the RBI Board to reject the present proposals. The Deepak Parekh Report should be put in the public domain.

Secondly, the government's cashless purchase of RBIs stake in SBI is clearly a case of the government simply plundering the RBI's assets without any compensation. An *amicus curiae* should challenge the proposal in the Supreme Court if the proposed amendment of the SBI is passed by Parliament. The visceral memories of the government would surely recall the striking down by the Supreme Court of the Bank Nationalisation Act of 1969 on the ground that the compensation did not meet the criteria of fairness. "Those who do not remember the mistakes of the past would be punished by the future" (Zarathushtra).

India Incorporated is stung by the mild increase in the dividend distribution tax from 12.5 per cent to 15.0 per cent. It is preposterous that final beneficiaries of dividends enjoy unlimited tax free facilities. The measure now taken is appropriate as also the enhancement of the dividend distribution tax for money market and liquid mutual funds.

The Budget is curiously silent on the 80 C tax deduction and the operational details of the transition from EEE to EET. Any further delay in clarifying this matter would result in chaos in the future.

From the Finance Minister's post-Budget interviews it would appear that the fisc would concentrate on growth with distributive justice, without aggravating inflation and the RBI would focus on containing inflation. This is how it should be.

Divya Bhaskar—March 5, 2007.

33 Goodbye to Income Tax Refunds

The government has, in recent years, made heroic efforts to simplifying the income tax returns so that the *aam aadmi* does not face difficulties in submitting returns and, more importantly, in getting tax refunds. Sincere efforts were made to expedite refunds and a Saral Form was introduced which, over time, proved to be Non-Saral. Those not eligible to fill the Saral Form could fill the 2D Form which was reasonably easy to file. At this stage most individuals could file their returns without outside help.

The problem started when the tax authorities rightly went after the tax cheaters and for the financial year 2005-06 (Assessment Year 2006-07) introduced a new Form 2F with cash flow requirements. The new Form created an uproar and the government, assessing the political economy of a fall out, widely withdrew the 2F Form.

Undeterred by the experience, the Revenue Department pursued the objective of simplifying and streamlining the income tax returns and for 2007-08 a new set of eight income tax returns (ITRs) have been introduced, but only for Assessment Year 2007-08 i.e., year ending March 31, 2007.

The difficulty with these new forms is not so much the information called for but the underlying approach of the Income Tax Department of total faith in the infallibility of the giant computer of the department. It is as if the government has passed an edict: "Every citizen must be computer savvy or else he has no right to exist."

The authorities expect all individual tax payers to download the ITR forms and make suitable "space adjustments" to tailor the form to the individual tax payer's needs. The acid test for an appropriate ITR form is that an individual with a modicum of knowledge should be able to fill the form. Illustratively, ITR-2, which most individuals will have to fill, is so intricate that individuals would just not be able to fill the form on their own.

Anticipating these difficulties, the authorities have introduced a system of Tax Return Prepares (TRPs). Who are these TRPs and where are they located and have they really been trained? Moreover, if the TRPs commit mistakes, would the tax authorities refrain from penalising tax payers? Of course, the response would be to check the Tax Return Preparer Scheme, 2006 dated November 26, 2006. If you do not have a copy of the scheme, go onto the Net. If you are not computer savvy, tough luck.

The real woes of the tax payer relate to establishing credits for tax deduction at source (TDS). With the Income Tax Department's obsession with computerisation, which by itself is desirable, it should not be relentlessly pursued to the point where tax payers with impeccable track records are harassed and denied their legitimate TDS credits.

One of the basic tenets of the new ITR Forms is that no attachments are allowed. To insist that Form 16 or Form 16A cannot be attached is going to hurt a large number of income tax payers. The authorities are no doubt aware that tax deductors invariably issue the TDS Certificate without stating the PAN of the tax payer. As a result, the giant computer would reject the claim of the tax payer.

It is well known that the requirement is that refunds have to be given before the end of the next financial year; this is observed more in the breach. Instead, a notice comes to the tax payer that he/she has not declared the PAN while investing in bank fixed deposits, savings bonds, mutual funds or equity shares or that the PAN is incorrectly indicated in the return—this is really a red herring.

I would request the new Revenue Secretary, Shri P.V. Bhide, and the new Chairman Central Board of Direct Taxes (CBDT) Shri B.M. Singh, to consider the following:

(i) Tax payers should be allowed to attach copies of advance tax and self-assessment tax paid.

(ii) Tax payers should be allowed to attach Form 16 or 16A as evidence of TDS. As per present instructions, the income tax officers, while accepting the ITR forms will tear out the Form 16/16A certificates and return them to the tax payer. Senior CBDT officials have said that Form 16/16A can be attached. But has the CBDT informed all offices that they should accept Form 16/16A? Likewise, attachments on Section 80 C and Section 80 G deduction support documents should be accepted by the income tax offices. An immediate notification is imperative.

(iii) If a tax payer provides evidence of a TDS in Form 16/16A but the deductor does not reveal the PAN of the tax payer, the authorities should not penalise the tax payer; rather they should take action against the tax deductor.

(iv) Income tax payers should be allowed to attach a detailed statement in support of their returns, as the space provided in the form is inadequate.

Finally, I would appeal to the new Revenue Secretary, Shri P.V. Bhide, to show compassion and not punish honest tax payers for the shortcomings of the tax deductors or the deficiencies in the tax department's giant computer.

Divya Bhaskar—June 25, 2007.

34 The Travails of Marginal Income Tax Payers

There is an erroneous view that the burden of income tax in India is significantly higher than in most other countries. A look at the maximum rates of income tax shows that the card rate in India of 30 per cent is among the lowest in the world. Canada (29 per cent) and Malaysia (28 per cent) are countries with lower rates. In most other major developed and emerging countries, the rates are significantly higher and a number of countries have rates of 40 per cent or over—Australia, China, Germany, UK, Israel, Spain, South Africa and France. The pertinent question that arises is why there is so much discontent among individuals, particularly marginal income tax payers. The problem is not with the tax rate but the tax administration.

We are still governed by the Income Tax Act 1961, as amended from time to time. The maze of amendments is such that it is virtually impossible for the *aam aadmi* to understand the tax system and small tax payers need professional help. True, the government has made sincere efforts to ease the burden of tax payers and introduced a scheme of Registered Income Tax Preparers. While this is a commendable effort, the scheme raises a number of doubts. What is the credibility of the registered Income Tax Preparers? What happens if the Income Tax Preparer makes a mistake—obviously, the rap comes on the tax payer. Where are these Registered Income Tax Preparers and are they sufficient in number to cover the bulk of income tax payers?

The Finance Minister has said that that there would be a new Direct Tax Code which would demystify the provisions of the Income Tax Act and the new Act was to come into effect from April 1, 2008, but there does not seem any light at the end of the tunnel.

For the financial year ended March 31, 2007, small income tax payers were faced with a totally new system. It was claimed that the super giant computer of the Tax Department would be able to store all the relevant information relating to a tax payer and so no attachments were permitted such as Tax Deduction Certificates (TDS) or evidence in support of 80C deductions.

The Central Board of Direct Taxes (CBDT) had directed that all income tax refunds up to Rs. 25,000 should be completed by the end of September 2007 and all other refunds should be completed by the end of November 2007. It is commendable that about 20 lakh applications have been completed and Rs. 4,300 crore has been refunded. It is reported that the processing has been faster as compared with earlier years. So far so good, but we need to deal with the ground realities.

More often than not, income tax payers do not receive refunds within the stipulated period. Invariably, the tax payer gets an innocuous notice that the PAN number does not tally with the super giant computer or that the tax payer has bought the government's Savings Bond without revealing the PAN number. When the tax payer submits a copy of the Bond Application Form which shows that the PAN number was indeed revealed, comes a further query that the signature does not tally. In short, there are lakhs of marginal tax payers who do not get their refunds for years.

A pertinent question is why do tax payers pay excess tax and then clamour for refunds. The fact is that in many cases this is involuntary. The individual is a marginal tax payer and multiple agencies deduct tax at source at 20 per cent plus surcharge and education cess. Again, such tax payers as are at the margin cannot take the risk of filling the Forms 15G or 15H.

There should be a failsafe mechanism to ensure that all income tax refunds relating to years prior to the year ended March 31, 2007 are cleared and refunds paid. There is a need for an effective monitoring system. The Central Board of Direct Taxes (CBDT) should undertake random *in cognito* visits to the income tax offices to assess compliance at the grassroots level. Furthermore, there should be a system under which all tax refund claims up to say Rs. 25,000 for the financial year ended March 31, 2006 can be reported by the tax payer to a Central Registry regarding their claims and this information should be put in the public domain. There should be a system under which refunds up to Rs. 25,000 should be automatically paid within six months of the date of filing the return.

There has to be an honour system where tax returns upto a stipulated taxable income, of say Rs. 5 lakh, are cleared on receipt without any detailed scrutiny and the refund should be immediately paid. The motto should be "Refund first and Scrutiny later". Of course false claims should be subject to severe penalties.

The authorities should consider disseminating a "Code on Government's on Refunds to Small Income Tax Payers" modelled on the Code introduced by the Banking Codes and Standards Board of India. Till then, marginal income tax payers can only hope and pray for income tax refunds.

Divya Bhaskar—October 29, 2007.

35 Union Budget 2008-09

Curtain Raiser

The Union Budget for 2008-09 is some time away but key elements of the jigsaw puzzle start falling into place from the previous November.

A number of key budget indicators and targets are set out as a percentage of the nominal gross domestic product (GDP). Yet, the Budget Speech does not explicitly state what nominal (i.e., current prices) GDP is used. Using the figures revealed in the Budget, it is possible to work out the nominal GDP growth built into the Union Budget exercise. It would be no surprise if the Budget for 2008-09 is based on a nominal GDP growth of 12-13 per cent. But what is not revealed is the underlying vital components *viz.*, the real GDP growth and the inflation rate. As part of greater transparency and internal consistency, it would be a major improvement if the Finance Minister were to formally set out in the Budget Speech, the underlying projection for nominal GDP growth in 2008-09 along with the components of real GDP growth and the inflation rate. The government would be well advised to take the stance that it would be best to work with an 8 per cent real GDP growth and a 4 per cent inflation rate. The reason for caution on real GDP growth in 2008-09 would be that there are signs of slowdown in production of consumer durables and non-durables and intermediate goods while capital goods output continues to show buoyancy. There are typical signs of impending cyclical dislocation and there could be the possible danger of inter-sectoral mal-investment, with excess capacity in some sectors and deficient capacity in other sectors. Typically, at the upper turning point of the business cycle, there are sectoral supply-demand mismatches which, if unattended to, could result in a sharp downturn of overall output.

There is a viewpoint that we should abandon the gross fiscal deficit and the revenue deficit targets. It is argued that the fisc is no longer a drag on the economy and that the government should abrogate the

Fiscal Responsibility and Budget Management (FRBM) Act. While the international crude oil price is heading towards US$ 100 per barrel, in India we have not allowed a pass through of even the earlier increase in crude prices which shows that the current inflation rate gives a false sense of complacency. Furthermore, there are strong trends which point to increased prices of food and other commodities. In such a situation, it would be foolhardy to provide a fiscal stimulus.

In a seminal paper by Dr. C. Rangarajan, co-authored by Dr. D. Subbarao, (*Economic Times*, February 19 and 20, 2007), it is cogently argued that we should persevere with a cautious fiscal policy. The paper argues that delivery on the FRBM targets is critical to sustaining the current growth momentum. Since macroeconomic stability is the bedrock of sustained growth, low inflation, stable interest rates and a comfortable balance of payments position are critically dependent on redressing fiscal imbalances.

The debt-GDP ratio of the Centre and states was 79.5 per cent in 2005-06. What is worrisome is that apart from the existence of the gross fiscal deficit, there is, in India, the existence of a revenue deficit which means that borrowed money is being used for current consumption like payment of salaries and pensions, subsidies and interest payments. In other words, a substantial part of the gross fiscal deficit does not build up investments but is used for current consumption. It is in this context that the FRBM Act targets need to be scrupulously adhered to in 2008-09 *viz.*, a zero revenue deficit and a 3 per cent gross fiscal deficit. A revenue deficit does create an inter-generation burden in that the current spending passes on the pain of debt servicing to the next generation.

There is euphoria in some circles that the fiscal situation has turned the corner in the current financial year (2007-08). The data for the early months of 2007-08 are a cause of worry. In the period up to August 2007, the revenue deficit is clearly out of control as the deficit is 75 per cent of the full year's revenue deficit. Even this figure is arrived at by blatant jugglery of accounts. While the budget documents for 2007-08 show the profit transfer by RBI to government on the sale of State Bank of India as a capital receipt, the accounts up to August 2007 show this profit transfer as non-tax revenue. Hence, the true revenue deficit up to August 2007 is

130 per cent of the full year's budget estimate. Furthermore, the gross fiscal deficit is camouflaged by quasi-fiscal deficits (i.e., extra budgetary expenditures) which would be at least 2 per cent of GDP for the Centre.

The revenue deficit would further deteriorate with the burden of the Market Stabilisation Scheme Bonds which, at the present ceiling of Rs. 250,000 crore, would imply an annual interest cost of almost Rs. 19,000 crore. The impact of the Sixth Pay Commission would only worsen the revenue deficit and jeopardise the FRBM targets.

Hence, the fiscal correction which is talked about by some commentators is illusory and it would be dangerous in Budget 2007-08 to yield to the pleas for fiscal expansion, which apart from being inappropriate from the viewpoint of fiscal prudence, would also be embarrassing to the government from a political economy viewpoint.

Divya Bhaskar—November 26, 2007.

36 The Personal Income Tax Regime is Iniquitous

Although the income tax regime has been streamlined from time to time, the basic structure remains a maze. While the promised Income Tax Code is expected to rationalise the system, it is unclear whether the iniquity in the area of personal income tax will be addressed.

The present overall burden (30 per cent maximum income tax plus surcharge and education cess) is clearly reasonable in comparison with a number of countries. The problem, however, is that, over time, *inter se* iniquity has crept into the system. The problem lies in the manner in which the system of exemption works. A basic principle of public finance is that all income should be treated as income for tax purposes but large tracts of income fall outside the tax net.

The avowed objective is to bring down the exemptions and deductions which is unexceptionable, but this has had perverse effects.

To encourage investments in certain instruments, the initial amount of investment is exempt (E), the income earned thereon is exempt (E) but on maturity or sale of the asset the entire amount is taxed (T); this is called the EET system. It is well taken that a tax payer gets the exemption today but only adds to his taxable income at a future date which is a major advantage because of the inflation factor. It is also recognised that many of the industrial countries follow the EET system. But before we ape the system prevailing in certain industrial countries, we need to take note of the ground realities in India. We cannot forget that a large proportion of the population does not enjoy social security. It is precisely for this reason that the government has thought of a national pension scheme for all persons above a certain age who meet certain income and other criteria.

Under the present system there is a provision for a deduction of Rs. one lakh from taxable income under Section 80 C and while earnings are also exempt from income, any withdrawals are subject to tax in the year of withdrawal. For those who do not have proper social security, the tax burden hits them precisely when income falls and the individual is unable to bear the tax burden.

When the EET system was announced a couple of years ago there was intense public debate about the operational snags and therefore, the Kannan Committee was appointed. It is unfortunate that the public has not been informed about the status of the EET system i.e., whether the system is to be introduced or has it been shelved. Meanwhile, tax payers are merrily enjoying the 80 C exemption. It would appear from the official silence that there would be insurmountable operational problems.

It would only be fair that the authorities make it explicitly clear in the next budget as to their intentions. Implementing the EET system in the financial year 2008-09 would not be feasible from a political economy viewpoint. To cut through the morass of confusion, it would be best to abandon the EET system till a reasonable social security system is in place, but simultaneously the 80 C deduction from income up to Rs. one lakh should be withdrawn. As such, no tax deduction from income should be allowed at the time of investment (T) but any accruals of income would be exempt (E) and the withdrawal should be exempt (E). In other words, there would be a TEE system. While abolishing the 80 C exemption the existing basic exemption limits for various categories—general, women and senor citizens should be appropriately raised.

The total exemption of dividend income from income for purposes of income tax is a sheer atrocity. Exempting persons with phenomenal dividend income running into crores of rupees is on the basis that the corporate would have paid tax so the dividend recipient should not be taxed once again, is totally erroneous. On this basis every salary earner should be allowed to carry a card that he has paid his income tax so when he buys his/her groceries no further taxes can be imposed. Exempting dividend distributed by a corporate to individuals on the basis that the company pays a dividend distribution tax does not hold. Those not in the taxable bracket bear a high burden while those at the maximum bracket get away. The lobby for tax free status on dividends is far too powerful and they will never allow a total withdrawal of the facility. One approach would be a slow battle of attrition under which there is a small increase in the rate of dividend distribution tax. There must be some fiscal equity between various risk bearing instruments. At present, the odds are all in favour of the highest income brackets while putting a cruel burden on the middle and lower income brackets. A government which claims it is for the *aam aadmi* should be more sensitive on these issues. Two alternatives could be considered: (i) The existing company dividend distribution tax could be left unchanged but the long-term capital gains tax could be 10 per cent and short-term capital gains tax raised to 20 per cent. (ii) The existing dividend distribution tax could be raised by 5 percentage points above its existing level (there are different slabs for different instruments).

The ultimate objective should be to have a fair and efficient tax regime and not a regime totally favouring the powerful few. The taxation of dividends and capital gains needs a wide and fair debate.

Divya Bhaskar—December 10, 2007.

37 Distributive Justice Should be the Theme of the Budget

On February 29, 2008, the Union Finance Minister would unfold the last budget of the UPA government. This year's budget would no doubt test the skills of the policymakers. The key inputs of the budget would, by now, already have been settled and any articulation in the media would be merely an expression of hopes and fears.

At the macro level, unlike in a number of countries which are talking about fiscal expansion, there is no fiscal space in India for expansion. It is essential that the commitments under the Fiscal Responsibility and Budget Management Act (FRBM) are adhered to in 2008-09. In this context, it is imperative that in 2008-09 the union government revenue deficit is eliminated and the gross fiscal deficit is contained within 3 per cent of GDP. It is important that the fiscal correction is genuine and not achieved by a larger quasi-fiscal deficit under which expenditures are moved outside the budget through instruments like oil bonds. If the fiscal commitments under the FRBM for 2008-09 cannot be transparently met it would be better to admit such shortfalls rather than sweep the dust under the carpet. One of the basic tenets of the FRBM is transparency but what is unfortunate is that independent evaluation of the adherence to fiscal transparency has not been provided for. The change in ownership of the State Bank of India from RBI to government is a glaring case of misrepresentation of the fiscal performance. If the SBI transaction had been properly recorded, the revenue deficit would have been much larger.

There are the fashions of the time. Each time the government undertakes a programme to alleviate the suffering of the masses, it is labelled as "populist", yet major fiscal concessions for the elite are justified on the ground that it is "productive". In the Budget for 2008-09, the government should give prominence to distributive justice.

With savings at 37 per cent and investments at 38.5 per cent of GDP, India now has the prerequisites for sustaining a real growth of the economy of 8.5 per cent; this would admittedly be lower than the 9 per cent plus growth rates of the past two years. Nonetheless to say, a 8.5 per cent growth rate should be considered as a very satisfactory achievement; sage Rangarajan has endorsed this viewpoint. We need to abjure from a fiscal stimulus which would only worsen the inflationary situation. The best anti-poverty programme is the control of inflation. It would be preferable to have an 8 per cent real growth with 4 per cent inflation rather than a 9 per cent growth with a 6 per cent inflation. The economy is growing at a rate close to its potential and a fiscal stimulus would contribute more to inflation than growth.

Receipts under direct taxes have increased from Rs. 105,000 crore in 2003-04 to an estimated Rs. 300,000 crore in 2007-08. While direct taxes are increasingly the tax of the future, there is a strong case for *inter se* equity. One of the arguments put forth is that the direct tax net is very narrow and there should be a much wider coverage of the population contributing to direct taxes. This argument could be carried to an extreme absurdity. Given the inflation drift, the costs of administering tax collections from relatively low income groups and above all distributive justice, there is a case for raising the basic exemption limit from Rs. 1.1 lakh to Rs. 1.5 lakh, with corresponding higher exemption limits for women and senior citizens. A basic exemption limit of Rs. 1.5 lakh per annum would be equivalent to a monthly income of a little over Rs. 12,000 which, in this day and age, is a very modest income which deserves to be exempt from income tax. If large and unlimited exemptions are given to high net worth individuals, it is only fair that the individuals in the lowest tax bracket are also provided some relief.

To get out of the confusion of the proposed exempt exempt tax (EET) system, under which all withdrawals of capital and interest are to be added to income for tax purposes, the present Section 80 C tax deduction could be scrapped and Rs. 1 lakh added to the basic exemption limit, which could then be raised to Rs. 2.5 lakh, with corresponding increases for women and senior citizens.

The percipient, Mr. T.N. Pandey, with his past experience at the Central Board of Direct Taxes, has pointed out that the total exemption of long-term capital gains tax from income tax is not justified, the unlimited exemption of dividend income is unconscionable and the present dividend distribution tax is regressive. With such large benefits to the upper income groups, the Finance Minister could surely raise the basic income tax exemption limit.

Divya Bhaskar—February 12, 2008.

38 Union Budget 2008-09

Goodies for All But Who Will Pay

The Union Budget for 2008-09 presented by the Finance Minister is a hoopla with prizes for all. It is remarkable in the extent of giveaways. Admittedly, each giveaway is preceded by a clear rationale. While one may have some reservations about the fiscal gymnastics, in fairness it must be said that the government has clearly announced that the Fiscal Responsibility and Budget Management Act (FRBM) stipulation of a zero revenue deficit in 2008-09 would not be attained, even though the fiscal deficit could be within the stipulated figure of 3 per cent of GDP. There are a number of major items of expenditure which have not been provided for, such as the agricultural debt relief scheme and the Pay Commission award. The Finance Commission would be requested to take a realistic review of the FRMB targets.

The government has to be credited for stating in the Budget Speech that there are significant liabilities in terms of oil, food and fertiliser bonds and that it is necessary to bring these liabilities into the fiscal accounting. This is a right step towards fiscal transparency. Again, the nominal GDP projection for 2008-09 is explicitly built into the "the Budget at a Glance" and this reduces the jiggery-pokery.

The burden of the loan waiver is estimated at around Rs. 60,000 crore which has not been provided for in the budget; the fiscal impact would, however, be felt over a three-year period. It is not as if the lowest income group should not be provided relief. Rather it is a question whether there could be a more equitable scheme which is not biased against small farmers who have paid off their loans despite facing extreme deprivation. For instance, farmers with a certain area of land could be provided an outright subsidy while those with loans outstanding would be required to use the subsidy to repay the bank loans. Those who have paid off their loans would be at an advantage, under such a scheme. This way, the argument against debt waivers would be more muted as the government subsidy would be neutral as between defaulters and those who repay their loans. As such, the future incentive to default would be minimised.

There were great anticipations that individual income tax payers would be provided significant relief. The raising of the basic exemption in the case of individuals, women and senior citizens is welcome especially as the tax slabs are less steep than hitherto. Quite appropriately, the Finance Minister has increased the basic exemption limit rather than increasing the Section 80 C deduction. As part of an equitable rationalisation, the Section 80 C deduction of Rs. one lakh, could have been totally abolished and the basic exemption limit raised correspondingly. Channelling savings into select instruments through fiscal incentives is not the most efficient way of operating the tax administration.

The removal of the tax deduction at source (TDS) for corporate bonds, as recommended by the R.H. Patil Committee, is welcome as it would enable easier trading of these bonds. There is an anomalous situation wherein the 8 per cent Savings Bond (taxable) is subject to a rigorous TDS. Surely, the government readily knows who has invested in these bonds. One would hope that the Central Board of Direct Taxes (CBDT) would look into this piquant situation wherein the government discriminates against its own instrument. Surely, the CBDT knows the kind of persons investing in these bonds—an analysis would readily bring out that most investors are senior citizens or persons on relatively low income. This anomaly needs to be quickly rectified.

The increase in the short-term capital gains tax is most appropriate as it reduces volatility in financial markets.

The boost to reverse mortgage by not treating the transaction as a transfer and the stream of income received by the house owner as free from income tax will be of tremendous advantage to those senior citizens who are asset rich but income poor.

There is a tinge of sadness that a large number of individuals who are eligible for refunds of income tax do not get their dues for years on end and have to approach the concerned officers on bended knees seeking refunds. If greater tax compliance is the objective it should equally apply to refunds. A system should be introduced wherein the refund sought by a taxpayer up to a stipulated amount should be automatically paid within, say a period of six months, after filing of the return. In cases where refund claims are found to be false, appropriate penalties could be imposed. Thus, the individual's trust in the tax administration and the tax authority's trust in individuals should be two-way.

As Tony Blair said in his Mais Lecture sometime in the early 1990s, "It is no longer a matter of giveaways before General Elections, but how credible a party's programme is." These are questions which the electorate is bound to ask and this needs cool and collected cogitation and not mere rhetoric.

Divya Bhaskar—March 10, 2008.

39 The Economic Survey 2007-08

A Futuristic Document

The Economic Survey for 2007-08 is an outstanding document in that it bites the bullet on what needs to be done by way of reforms in the medium-term to enable India to be in the forefront of growth in an international context. Kudos to the economists of the Minister of Finance.

The Survey draws on the historical experience that there have been about a dozen medium/large countries which have averaged a GDP growth rate of 9 per cent for, say a decade, but only one-half of these countries have continued to grow at the same pace for two decades. While the media and India Incorporated to gaga on the high growth rate of the past few years, the Survey does well to highlight that we have a lot of hard work to undertake to keep the momentum going. The Survey promises no facile solutions and focuses on the harder issues of reforms.

High GDP growth attracts foreign capital looking for profitable investment opportunities. In a positive cycle, the inflows find these profitable opportunities. If the growth opportunities do not materialise fast enough, there is pressure on the currency to appreciate with accumulation of forex reserves, which are then followed by monetary expansion and inflation. The Survey posits that the surge in capital inflows, including FDI will continue in the medium-term. Capital inflows as a percentage of GDP may decline slightly in 2008 because of the sub-prime crisis in the developed countries. Nonetheless, the capital inflows will be excessive. The eventual solution to excessive capital inflows lies in deepening productivity gains and keeping inflation rates and interest rates close to international levels.

The Survey rightly stresses that in earlier years inflation was largely a structural problem of specific shortages, particularly of agricultural and agro-based products. In more recent years, the opening up of the economy has made inflation management a more complex task. Thus, there could be inflation generated by external impulses and it is here that a greater role needs to be assigned to monetary policy. The Survey recognises that if Indian real interest rates are significantly higher than international rates, there would be large short-term capital inflows. In this context a convergence of interest rates first requires a convergence of inflation rates but this is easier said than done. Apart from effectively tackling the major infrastructural bottlenecks, removing constraints to agricultural modernisation and increasing urban land supply are necessary. It is also vital to develop India's debt and currency markets. Developing financial markets with depth is perhaps the hardest part of the reform.

The Survey rightly pinpoints that the fiscal deficit has to be further reduced to widen the space for an effective monetary policy. A lower fiscal deficit is crucial to the convergence of Indian and international interest rates. The Survey urges the Finance Commission to consider setting the Fiscal Responsibility and Budget Management Act (FRBM) targets over the next five years and beyond.

The Survey candidly admits that the banking sector remains a "government oligopoly" despite the entry of foreign banks. The Survey is understandably silent on reduction of the public sector predominance in the banking sector. Furthermore, even while discussing the future "Policy Reform Options" the Survey discreetly stays clear of the issue of government giving up majority shareholding in public sector banks. This is an issue on which all governments since 1991 have been unable or unwilling to put through and the Survey wisely does not wish to be perilously left out on a limb. At best, the Survey refers to the need for "100 per cent FDI in Greenfield Private Rural-Agricultural Banks." So much for the much hyped opening up in March 2009 of the banking sector to foreign banks and consolidation of public sector banks.

While discussing the agenda for the next few years, the Survey refers to allowing FDI in retail trade and 100 per cent FDI in foreign branded specialised retail chains. In the insurance sector the Survey refers to the need for raising foreign equity to 49 per cent and select 51 per cent foreign equity for special category insurance companies exclusively dealing with rural residents.

The Survey is emboldened to argue that there is no option to hard work and raises the pertinent issue of increasing the work week under the

Factories Act to 60 hours from the present 48 hours, with a daily limit of 12 hours to meet seasonal demand. Unfortunately, we have prematurely aped the industrial countries in reducing the working week!

The Survey also discusses, at some length, the need for reforms in the states, which in some sense is the harder element of reforms.

All in all, the Economic Survey provides a veritable feast for serious-minded people who wish to give attention to reinforcing the reform process beyond 2009. The economists in the Ministry of Finance deserve to be complimented for their cerebral labours.

Divya Bhaskar—March 17, 2008.

40 Diwali Crystal Gazing

As we approach the New Year, we all have our hopes and aspirations. There is good news awaiting corporates, exporters, importers, capital market investors, non-resident Indians and high net worth individuals. Does anyone care for the *aam aadmi*? What we could attempt here is to relate likely developments in the economy during the next year from the viewpoint of the *aam aadmi*.

The economy is expected to grow at over 7.5 per cent. The authorities believe that we should become the fastest growing economy in the world and that millions of jobs would get created and the mass of unemployed would have unprecedented opportunities. Should we rejoice? There are dangers in the economy growing too fast—it is akin to running faster than one's legs can take and one falls in a heap. It is for this reason that wider counsels advise that an economy should not try to grow beyond its potential. The lessons to learn here is that if the economy grows too fast, we should get worried.

When an economy pushes beyond the limits to growth, what results is acceleration in inflation. Official estimates are that the inflation during the financial year April 2005 to March 2006 will be around 5-5.5 per cent. The inflation rate is already 4.6 per cent and is a cause for worry. There are a number of reasons for this inflation pressure. The banks are sitting on a mountain of liquidity and corporates have large excess funds. This puts pressure on inflation and misuse of credit.

The increase in international crude oil prices has not been fully passed on to consumers. The burden of a rise in international crude oil prices cannot be hidden in the economy. The government and/or the oil companies may bear the cost, but anyhow, the inflation will find its way into the economy.

The bad news is that inflation will be much higher than the authorities' estimate and the year could end with an inflation rate of over

7 per cent unless the authorities take strong and timely monetary and fiscal measures. The *aam aadmi* will feel the inflation impact more than others. We already have the onion price hike. A sharp spurt in wheat prices is likely. Fresh domestic wheat supplies will come only in May 2006 and present stocks are insufficient to tide over till April 2006. Imports may be undertaken to ease the bind. The Indian palate finds imported wheat inedible so consumers will chase scarce domestic wheat supplies and thereby wheat prices will skyrocket.

We are told, and correctly so, that if the economy has to grow, we need to increase investment and for that we need to step up savings. The household sector provides the bulk of savings in India and within the household sector's savings, the predominant part is savings in the form of bank deposits. Furthermore, the *aam aadmi* accounts for a major part of bank deposits. Now how does the fiscal-monetary system reward the saver in bank deposits? Let us assume that bank fixed deposits have a nominal interest rate of 6 per cent. With inflation at 5 per cent, the real rate of interest is very low or negative. Furthermore, say a depositor places a deposit of Rs. 100 for 5 years and the average rate of inflation is 5 per cent, in real terms the deposit is worth Rs. 78. In the year going forward, the depositor has to be prepared for negative real interest rates and large capital losses. Put bluntly, the monetary system is unfair to the *aam aadmi*.

The fiscal system is equally unfair. Tax concessions for bank depositors have been curtailed while tax bonanzas have been awarded to investors in mutual funds and companies.

The *aam aadmi* cannot afford to wallow in his misery. In a Diwali spirit, the system is forcing him to take risks.

First, the *aam aadmi* should try and encash on the housing boom. He should use all his fixed deposits to meet the down payment for a dwelling and borrow the rest.

Secondly, gold is the best hedge against inflation. The *aam aadmi* should shift from bank deposits to gold under a systematic investment plan. A rider here is to go in for gold proper and not jewellery.

Third, the *aam aadmi* should move from bank deposits to debt mutual funds.

If the authorities wish to beat bank depositors, the *aam aadmi* can also teach the authorities a lesson or two.

Finally, if the *aam aadmi* wishes to be more cheerful at the next Diwali, he should respond to the changing environment. A passive approach will only add to his woes. So let's hope that in the ensuing year, the *aam aadmi* will give an appropriate response to the policy-making *pundits*.

Divya Bhaskar—October 31, 2005.

IV

41 Apocalypse Awaits Small Savers

Governmental committees have for some time been working on overhauling the tax system for savings. It is argued that, at present, the contributions, interest and withdrawals are exempt from taxation at all three stages and that there should be one stage at which tax should be paid. Experts draw upon the experience of many countries to support this contention. In the Budget for 2005-06, the Finance Minister announced that from financial year 2005-06, all tax rebates and deductions from income would be withdrawn and a consolidated deduction of Rs. one lakh from income would be introduced covering a number of instruments. It was further indicated that all interest on these investments would be exempt from tax but withdrawals would be subject to tax.

The Government appointed the R. Kannan Committee to work out the modalities of the new system and the Committee has reportedly submitted its report.

Why should the saver worry about the tax at the withdrawal stage? A saver who saves say Rs. 10,000 per year would have saved a total of Rs. 1,50,000 in 15 years which, with interest could amount to at least Rs. 3,00,000. Now the saver's problem is that he would have to pay tax on the entire Rs. 3,00,000. This big blow would come when the saver is least able to bear it. It is likely that the saver would withdraw the amount as his income falls or ceases. Furthermore, if the saver has not been a taxpayer all these years and has not benefited from the tax concession, it is unfair that he has to suddenly bear a large tax burden. It is often nonchalantly argued that after all, the tax payer can always claim a refund of the tax deduction at source (TDS). Anyone who has tried to get a refund of TDS under the National Savings Scheme would have tales of woe. If a saver is a marginal/nil taxpayer, he would have difficulty in claiming 15G status of being not subject to TDS.

A forceful argument is that high net worth individuals are using the Public Provident Fund Scheme (PPF) as a tax shelter.

Before the Kannan Committee Report is implemented, it should be first put in the public domain. This is too important a matter to be settled within cloistered walls.

If the authorities are adamant on taxing withdrawals, withdrawals in phases could be permitted and that only withdrawals of say over Rs. 30,000 per annum could be subject to tax. The whole issue should be made to stand on its head i.e., tax the initial contribution as part of the income (or in other words do not provide any exemption for contributions), but exempt interest and the withdrawal. This makes sense as tax is collected today and not at a future date. Moreover, the lower income diligent saver is protected from a brutal tax.

Even in the case of fresh accounts after the transition, it is not reasonable to tax withdrawals. If the government is concerned about the quantum of withdrawals, the Chile model could be used wherein withdrawals are staggered.

The time is appropriate to come to grips with the basic problem of small savers. Why are they being targeted for punishment? We have almost come close to treating small savers as parasites. The idea seems to be to exterminate the small savers to expose large hoarders who are reportedly masquerading as small savers.

The government is on the cusp of a fundamental change for the tax treatment of small savings and, therefore, a careful and full public interaction is necessary. The public has the right to know what sort of transition is envisaged. One would presume that there would be a system of pre-zero accounts i.e., accounts before the new system is introduced which would be exempt from the new system. There would necessarily be a large amount of paper work. Surely, a PPF holder would not be told in the 15th year of his account that all withdrawals would be subject to tax. This would be patently unfair. At most, no credits (other than interest) should be allowed and withdrawals should be on existing terms. The Kannan Committee is undertaking measures which have implications for a large body of savers and the Committee should sympathetically look into the problems of savers and not restrict itself to mere procedures.

Now why is the small saver being subject to all these afflictions? Ostensibly, this is to make the system simpler. A simpler system should not be at the cost of small savers. Finally, the welfare of savers is vital and the Government should consider setting up a specific Commission on small savings under the leadership of a eminence gris.

Divya Bhaskar—November 14, 2005.

42 Severe Punishment for Small Savers

Ever since the Finance Minister, Mr. P. Chidambaram announced the budgetary measure on taxation of savings in February 2005, it sent shivers down the spines of small savers. The *pundits* have, no doubt, waxed eloquently about the merits of an exempt (savings), exempt (interest) and tax (withdrawals) saying that it is superior to a system which exempts from tax at all three stages.

In the 1980s, savings instruments the world over were benefiting from fiscal privilege (i.e., fiscal benefits were high and effective rates of return were very high). Moreover, the higher the income, the higher the return. Countries like the UK and Japan scrapped these large tax benefits. In India too, it was recognised that very high effective rates of return were unwarranted.

The whole system has come round to the emergence of low nominal rates and reduced fiscal concessions. The Union Budget for 2005-06 threw a bombshell in that a deduction from income was provided for the current year's savings under Section 80 C but the entire amount on withdrawal is to be subject to tax.

The vexatious issue is that what happens to the amount of principal and interest (including future interest) on investments made before the new system comes into force.

Of course we have the Kannan Committee Report which is understandably going to be under wraps till the February 2006 Budget is announced.

After announcing the fundamental change in taxation of savings, the details have not been fleshed out even 10 months after the Budget for 2005-06.

How do we tread through the maze of intricate issues? A fervent prayer would be that the government withdraws the 80 C legislation and transparently puts a discussion paper in the public domain. But all governments believe that the wisdom lies exclusively with the government, so such hopes are clearly misplaced.

Intelligent guesses/calculated leaks indicate that the authorities are favourably inclined to index the annual ceiling under 80 C with the inflation rate. Given the duration of the savings instrument, consideration should be given to adjust the withdrawal corpus for inflation. This would not be an outrageous suggestion as it is permissible in the case of long-term capital gains.

Another hope is that tax would be imposed only on contribution made under various schemes after March 31, 2006. In effect, the financial year 2005-06 would be a twilight zone wherein there would be no rebate (Section 88) or deduction (Section 80 C). This is because the government is aware that courts frown on retrospective legislation. First and foremost, the government should put the EET system in cold storage. Imagine a complex nature of calculations for a public provident fund (PPF) account opened after March 31, 2006. Such investors would have to preserve income tax records for 15 years. What happens to a PPF holder who does not avail the 80 C benefit? The bank where the account is kept will straight away deduct tax at source. It is essential for the tax authorities to understand the "bunching effect" of withdrawals. "Grandfathering"—exemption of all investments and interest before the cut-off date—is a well accepted principle of public finance.

Now look at a PPF account which is say half way through the 15 years period. There would need to be proportionate taxation at the time of withdrawal. To put it mildly, we would have a very messy tax system. The best course would be to keep PPF and other PF accounts and retirement benefits outside the EET. Early withdrawals which amount to misuse of the facility should, however, be subject to tax.

It is clear that while governments (past and present) have shouted from the rooftops that taxation for the salaried earners has been reduced, this can be controverted. Adjusted for inflation, the tax burden on salaried earners has gone up. Moreover, taxation is a relative matter. The corporate sector has been given many concessions. Reduction of long-term capital gains to nil and freeing dividends in the hands of the recipients from taxation are major concessions.

The uncertainty on the tax front has left genuine savers in the lurch. If the government wants to be fair to savers, it would give a holiday from EET upto March 2006 and come out with an unequivocal scheme of taxation.

It would be best to remove all tax concessions on investment in savings instruments and then there should be no question of taxation on withdrawal. The only incentive should be exclusion of interest from tax on specified retirement schemes. There is no social security in India and we are throttling savers, the old and the dispossessed.

Finally, the misadventure of EET should be rolled back.

Divya Bhaskar—January 9, 2006.

43 The Demat Scam and the Plight of Small Investors

In recent months much has been said and written about the scam in Demat shares and Initial Public Offers (IPOs). In more recent days there has been sharp focus on the action by the Securities and Exchange Board of India (SEBI) against Depository Participants (DPs) and Registrars. The issue about the regulatory action is now before the courts and the legal process will settle this appropriately.

What is of greater concern is what the fallout is on the mass of small investors. This is akin to the colonial approach of punishing the whole village for an individual person's violation. Blunt measures have been taken which are creating great hardships to the mass of small investors. There is a crying need to look into the problems of small investors.

DPs and mutual funds have come down heavily on small investors. A scare has spread through the small investor community that action will be taken against the entire community. It is therefore, necessary to discuss these concerns.

It is one thing, if thousands of Demat accounts are opened with a single first name with multitudes of permutations and combinations. If such cases come to light, appropriate action should no doubt be taken. When the depositories and the DPs come down heavily on the entire community of small investors it is a serious matter which needs public attention.

We first need to ask ourselves why small investors have multiple accounts. This is a result of the regulatory requirements. Historically, prior to the Demat facility coming into being, small holders perforce had multiple combinations of holdings. For instance, let us take a family of three, say, A, B and C and all the accounts have first name A. There would be various combinations: ABC, ACB, AB and AC. Now from a regulatory point all that is necessary is that the authorities can put a tracer on these accounts and what is relevant is that the DP should have adequate details of Party A. Party A could be legitimately expected to produce Income Tax Permanent Account Number (PAN). Initially DPs had reasonable information on account holders. The tax authorities initially issued PAN numbers but not PAN cards. Now small holders are being told that they must produce PAN cards and not merely PAN numbers. The issue of PAN cards has been tardy. The authorities would no doubt contend this view by saying that, now that a subsidiary of UTI is issuing PAN cards the work has been decentralised and a high-tech system has been put in place.

But let us look into the travails of aged small investors. A 94-year old totally bed ridden person is under the threat of rejection for a PAN card as his only available photograph is a black and white one. Or take the case of an 88-year old lady who faces a similar threat as although she has a colour photograph, with the ravages of ill health, her body is tilted to one side. It is believed that the PAN issuing authorities are prone to reject such applications.

If A and B have PAN cards and C has no gross income, C will have difficulty filing a nil return and even greater difficulty if he tries to file a return with gross zero income. In the upshot under the recent regulations A, B and C will not be allowed to operate their DP account.

The powers that be sometimes argue that small investors have no business to directly hold shares and that they should invest in mutual funds. But here comes another roadblock. Mutual fund will also not allow operations if all three parties do not have PAN cards.

To add to the woes of small holders, there is a roadblock on getting income tax refunds. Normally, if the return is filed within the stipulated time the refund has to be given by the end of the next financial year. Instead of a refund a computerised statement comes to the tax payer saying that the party has not given his PAN number or the PAN number is wrong. Now till all this is settled the tax payer is not entitled for his refund.

One recognise that erudite regulators can write intellectual tomes to debunk the cases set out in this column. But a more enlightened approach is for the authorities to do what is called "Mystery Shopping" to find out the grassroot realities through a random survey of operations at the field level. If this is not done we can no longer sing the hymn "Small is Beautiful" but accept the reality that "Small must Suffer". We are meant to be a civic society, so let us be fair to small investors.

Divya Bhaskar—May 15, 2006.

44 Market Crash and Small Investors

In recent months, the Indian stock market exhibited a wild and unprecedented rise and the Sensex reached 12,612 on May 10, 2006. In the aftermath of the bloodbath the Sensex fell by 17 per cent in a matter of 9 trading sessions. Over the past year, the Sensex doubled with the past three months reflecting a frenzy quite out of alignment with fundamentals.

The foreign institutional investors (FIIs), mutual funds (MFs), banks, other financial institutions and corporates all have the expertise to take care of themselves. The real issue is what happens to small investors? One frequently argued viewpoint is that the small investor has no business to be in the stock market and if a small investor does enter the stock market, he does so at his own risk and peril.

Before we dismiss the small investor, we need to go back to the origin of small investors in the Indian stock market. In India, traditionally, the small investor has accounted for a sizeable proportion of the total stock market. Till the 1950s, retail investors accounted for a sizeable portion of the government securities market. With the emergence of the captive market with statutory investments in government securities interest rates were artificially low and retail investors were forced out of the market.

It is argued that small investors should refrain from investing directly in the stock market but should come through mutual funds. For all the fanfare about mutual funds, their performance has not been exactly praiseworthy.

The swings in the stock market have essentially become an institutional game. The two major players are FIIs and MFs. The net investments of FIIs between May 10 and May 18, 2006 reflected a decline of Rs. 3,350 crore while MFs increased their holdings by Rs. 2,900 crore.

The pertinent question a small investor asks is whether it is time to quit the stock market. There are no ready answers. All the advice that one can offer is the old adage of buying and selling in small lots (small being defined in relation to an individual's holding). The small investor is left with the problem of determining an enduring upward or downward movement. To ensure that the small investor is not caught on the wrong side of market trends, small investors should not indulge in excessive transactions, and certainly not attempt to be day traders.

It is important that small investors get a reasonably sound assessment of the macro situation. Investors must recognise that the real rate of growth has been unprecedented, the rate of inflation is subdued, the external payments position is strong. The downside is the fiscal situation which continues to be worrisome. On balance, the overall macroeconomic situation is sound. Nevertheless, we need to recognise that global interest rates are likely to rise as inflationary pressures gather momentum in the leading industrial countries. This will have repercussions in India. But measured increases in interest rates in India should not create panic in the stock market.

As to the view that small investors have no business to be in the stock market, one has to bear in mind the Kindleberger formula for setting the equity-debt proportions: The equity percentage in a portfolio for an individual should be 100 minus his age.

Pundits who tell small investors to stay away from the equity market need to take note of a real life case. A gentleman retired in 1970 with a total savings of Rs. one lakh. The standard advice he would be given was that he should invest in debt instruments. On a 9 per cent return his annual income would be Rs. 9,000. The real value of the 1976 corpus of Rs. one lakh would today be Rs. 23,000 at a 5 per cent inflation rate. The gentleman and his wife are now totally bedridden and their expenses are Rs. 40,000 a month of which Rs. 35,000 goes towards medical expenses. The gentleman had an entirely equity portfolio with long-term investments which enabled him to meet these expenses without any help from any of his children.

The equity market is risky but a necessity for small investors. The equity market will rock but in the long-run yield good returns. The final advice to small investors is to stay invested in the equity market for the long-term and ignore the blips. Have a heart before turning away small investors from the equity market.

Divya Bhaskar—May 29, 2006.

45 Death and Financial Assets

Death is inevitable but it causes a financial trauma. Despite either or survivor clauses and nominations, families face problems.

Till a few years ago, death of a bank depositor was a nightmare. The moment a family reported the death of a depositor, the account was frozen, pending the identification of legal heirs. One very large bank devised a form in which all possible relatives were listed—parents, grandparents, children, grandchildren siblings, uncles, aunts, nephews, nieces, cousins and all similar in-laws. Now the family was required to produce an indemnity or guarantee from someone other than the listed relatives. In effect, the family was required to produce the indemnity or guarantee from a virtual stranger.

Governor Dr. Y.V. Reddy, with his passion for improved customer service for the *aam aadmi*, directed a Committee to simplify the procedures in banks relating to the death of a depositor. Probates, letters of administration, indemnities, guarantees, etc., were dispensed with in cases of either or survivor and other such accounts and where there were clear nominations. If, however, a court order restraining the bank was served, the bank would obviously abide by the court order.

Under the new procedure the surviving joint account holders (with either or survivor clause) or nominees are allowed to take away all balances in the account of the deceased. Having released all balances in the account of the deceased to the survivors or nominees, the bank would have discharged its liability and would not be required to be accountable for any in-fighting within the family. The simple logic being that if the joint holders, on their own could withdraw balances during the life time of the first holder, they should have unfettered right to withdraw the balance in the account on the death of the first holder. For pipeline flows a two-track approach was evolved. First, the inflows could be put in an escrow account of the deceased, pending resolution of the issue of legal heirs and secondly, the bank could return the funds to the sender (the choice would be that of the survivors). If the second or third holder expired, the name of the deceased would be simply struck off and the account allowed to continue. The simplified procedure has greatly reduced the trauma for the family of the deceased.

Similarly, bank locker procedures for dealing with the death of a locker holder have been simplified.

Now what happens to Demat accounts? Survivors are no longer at the mercy of individual company registrars as the survivors need to deal with the depository participant (DP). Dealing with the death of a client was a simple matter and the depository system was far ahead of the banking system. Then came the IPO frauds with multiple client accounts and the clampdown was severe. Now if A, B and C have a client account with a DP and B or C dies, the account of A is frozen. If there is another account of B, A and C, this account is also frozen. In both cases the surviving clients are required to open fresh accounts and are *de novo* required to be subject to Know Your Customer (KYC) norms as totally new customers.

Invariably, in a family, A and B would be old while C may be relatively younger. With increased longevity, these accounts are, in many cases, operated by a Power of Attorney (PA). If any one of A, B or C dies, a new account has to be opened and a new account cannot be opened with a Power of Attorney. It bears emphasising that NSDL, CSDL and DPs have handled such cases with great finesse and compassion to avoid discomfort to client account holders.

SEBI needs to consider setting up a small group of SEBI, NSDL, CSDL and a few DPs to simplify procedures in the case of death of a DP client. As a first step, if the second or third holder dies, the account could be left undisturbed with only the name of the deceased being struck off. If the first holder dies, and it is felt imperative to open a new account, the procedures should be simplified. In particular, the surviving DP client account holders should not be treated as strangers who have to be subject to rigorous KYC norms. The existing information of the clients should suffice for KYC norms. Surely, the regulators should be glad to receive the blessings of families visited by death.

The procedures for non-resident Indians opening DP client accounts need to be reviewed in the light of liberalising of the capital account by the Reserve Bank of India.

Divya Bhaskar—August 20, 2007.

46 Mutual Funds

Know Your Customer Should Not be a Licence to Kill Your Customer

As part of the wider objective of tracking down socially undesirable activities the world over, financial intermediaries are being required to collect certain standardised information from their clients and this is known as Know Your Customer (KYC) guidelines. The KYC guidelines were initially introduced for bank customers. During the past three years, lives of legitimate bank customers have been made miserable as there have been unnecessary hassles for customers. In response to protests from bank customers, the banks blamed the Reserve Bank of India (RBI) for setting out unreasonable guidelines and, in turn, the RBI blamed banks for poor implementation of the guidelines.

The tax authorities required information for transactions above specified limits for different types of transactions. The grand design was that the giant computer would track down all illegitimate transactions and the laudable objective of stopping nefarious activities would be achieved. All that happened was that relatively small income tax payers, invariably those seeking refunds, were subject to frivolous queries and inordinate delays in obtaining their dues. But hopefully these are transient difficulties which will soon pass.

The focus of KYC implementation has now shifted to mutual funds. Here, again, there is the grand design of feeding all information into a giant computer. Unlike in banks and depository participants (DPs) where customers were required to produce documents to the concerned bank or DP with whom the customer was dealing, in the case of mutual funds the customer is being buffeted very badly as the customer is required to satisfy a centralised agency with whom the customer has no relationship. In the case of mutual funds the KYC guidelines are being implemented without an element of sensitivity.

An investor may invest in more than one mutual fund and centralised information gathering does have some logic. The real life problems faced by mutual fund investors would have been alleviated had their been a system of the information being filtered through the investor's bank or DP.

The hassles faced by an investor are poignantly brought out by a real life case to which I have direct experience. An investor in a mutual fund opted to invest through the bank branch where he had a bank account. The bank branch, which was the broker, forwarded the application form and while doing so, required the investor to meet KYC requirements in a separate form giving details of the PAN card, proof of address and details of the bank account. On receipt of the cheque the mutual fund encashed the cheque and confirmed to the investor via an Account Statement confirming the holding of units in the concerned scheme. The Account Statement also recorded the PAN card number and as and when dividends were paid (in a monthly income scheme), the investor received dividends directly into his bank account.

So far so good, but that's when the music started and the investor received a surprise bombshell. The transfer agent of the mutual fund sent the investor a "KYC-Rejection Intimation" indicating "Status-KYC Failed". It was also indicated that "till the KYC is completed for all holders, further purchases will not be permitted in the folio". It is pertinent to clarify that all holders had filled the KYC form separately and provided all the required details. What is not clarified is whether the investor can redeem his investment or is the asset frozen? The communication further says that "for the convenience of investors in mutual funds, all mutual funds have made special arrangements with CDSL Ventures Ltd. (CVL) a wholly owned subsidiary of Central Depository Services (India) Ltd. (CDSL)". It is further stated that "application form for complying with KYC will be available from their Points of Service". The transfer agent's letter further says that "we request you to contact officers of mutual funds, registrars and mutual fund distributors (ARN Holders)". In the present case the investor approached the ARN Holder, which was the investor's bank through whom the investment was made, but the ARN Holder was not in a position to provide any explanation to the investor. As for the Points of Service (POS), there is no information provided as to where the POS is located. What is more telling is that the investor is not told why the investor has the ignominy of being labelled "Status-KYC Failed".

The purpose of setting out this painful episode is with the hope that the woes of investors in mutual fund would be addressed. SEBI, the Association of Mutual Funds of India (AMFI), the CSDL Ventures, select mutual funds and their registrars and select ARN Holders could quickly remedy the position so that the Know Your Customer guidelines do not become a licence to Kill Your Customer.

Divya Bhaskar—April 28, 2008.

V

47 New Initiatives in Banking Customer Service

The issue of customer service has dogged the Indian banking system for decades. Despite several attempts, the quality of customer service provided has not been up to the mark.

The Banking Ombudsman Scheme was first introduced in 1995 and subsequently amended in 2002 and 2006. The central feature of the scheme is that bank customers having a grievance, which is not satisfactorily resolved by the concerned bank, would have recourse to the Banking Ombudsman. While a number of Banking Ombudsman have been appointed for specific regions, the volume of complaints appears to be very low. Absence of complaints does not mean that there are no complaints. The sad fact is that most customers are afraid to complain.

Dr. Y.V. Reddy in his first policy statement, after taking over as Governor, made improved customer service to the *aam aadmi* as a key objective of the Reserve Bank of India. As part of this attempt, the Governor set up a Committee on Procedures and Performance Audit on Public Services (2004). The Committee's findings were that there were serious deficiencies in customer service and that there was a need to bring about a fundamental change in the overall approach to customer service and what was required was a change in the mind set of players. The Committee was of the view that there had been a disenfranchisement of the depositors and customers had been shorn off their fundamental rights. The late Mr. M.R. Pai, a champion of the bank customers said, "The biggest asset on the balance sheet of banks today is the ignorance of customers of their own rights and their reluctance to fight for them." The Committee felt that the intent of the policy is invariably diluted in the content of the policy and furthermore, procedures totally derail the policy objectives.

The RBI moved with great alacrity to rectify individual deficiencies pointed out by the Committee. The Governor, however, felt that there was a need to evolve an effective mechanism to locate and rectify systemic deficiencies.

In response to the Governor's directions, the Committee studied the institutional mechanisms evolved in a few major countries. The Committee was of the view that the provisions of an institutional framework that evaluates and oversees the absence of the code of conduct by banks would exert healthy virtuous pressure on the banks. The Committee recommended the setting up of the Banking Codes and Standards Board of India (BCSBI) as an independent organisation fully funded by the RBI.

The RBI accepted the basic recommendations of the Committee and set up the BCSBI as a society, which was registered on February 18, 2006. The management of the BCSBI has been entrusted to a seven member Governing Council under the Chairmanship of Smt. K.J. Udeshi, who was till recently part of the top management of the RBI. Other members of the Governing Council are Shri M.G. Bhide (banker), Shri M.M. Chitale (chartered accountant), Shri R.K. Krishna Kumar (service industry), Shri S. Divakara (depositors' representative), Shri S.R. Kolarkar (legal) and Shri Vinay Baijal (Chief General Manager—RBI) who will be the Chief Executive Officer. The Governing Council has a powerful inter-disciplining team which should be able to lay the foundation of a strong viable organisation to bring about effective correction of systemic deficiencies by monitoring compliance with Codes and Standards which banks agree to.

The Governor, at the inaugural meeting of the Governing Council, pledged full financial support for the Board for the first five years. The registration of banks with the BCSBI would provide greater supervisory comfort to the RBI. The Governor stressed that while it was hoped that the unleashing of competition in the context of liberalisation would ensure better customer service, these hopes have been belied. The BCSBI is expected to fill an institutional gap in the assessment of the performance of banks *vis-à-vis* the Codes and Standards based on established best practices.

While the Banking Ombudsman Scheme addresses individual complaints, the BCSBI would be a quasi-regulatory organisation dedicated to improving the quality of customer service.

An outline of the operation of the BCSBI was set out by the Chairperson Smt. K.J. Udeshi in a speech at the Bankers' Training College, RBI on "Banking Codes and Standards—An Indian Perspective" (February 2006). The Board is a collaborative effort between the RBI and the banking industry with the objective of promoting good banking practices by setting minimum standards, increasing transparency, achieving higher operating standards and above all promoting cordial banker-customer relationship which would foster confidence of the *aam aadmi* in the banking system.

The Indian Banks Association (IBA) in consultation with the member banks is working out a detailed Code of Banking Practices specifically tailored to the requirements of individual customers. The banks would have the ownership of the Code. The BCSBI, in turn, would assess whether the banks are indeed doing what they say. There would be a covenant between the banks and the BCSBI on adherence to the Code. The BCSBI would set out detailed guidance notes on the Code and enunciate the Compliance Policy and Disciplinary Policy. The BCSBI would appoint Field Managers who would report on actual field visits and variance between the Compliance Reports filed by the banks and the observations from the field visits would be taken up with banks for corrective action.

The BCSBI would exert healthy moral pressure on banks to adopt and comply with minimum self-imposed banking Codes and Standards. Thus, cases of infringements would go through a myriad of processing and there would not be any peremptory action by the BCSBI.

The sanction by the BCSBI would be in the form of naming banks and details of the breach, instruction to banks on remedial action, warning or reprimand and public censure. The extreme step would be cancellation of registration with the BCSBI. The central objective would be collaborative remedial action rather than penal measures. At long last, there would be an institution exclusively dedicated to the interests of the *aam aadmi's* interface with the banking system.

Divya Bhaskar—April 17, 2006.

Dr. Reddy stressed that the hesitation of customers to switch banks should not be considered as a certificate of good customer service. In this context Governor Reddy cautioned banks against exorbitant charges as it would be deemed to be undue enrichment. He questioned the validity of contracts between unequal parties and drew attention to a recent Supreme Court judgement regarding the non-enforcability of a contract between unequal partners. He emphasised that when the RBI considers customer service it will focus on the *aam aadmi*. One hopes that the RBI and the BCSBI will tilt the level playing field five degrees in favour of the bank customers, particularly the *aam aadmi*.

July 1, 2006 is a landmark in that the RBI, the banks and the BCSBI have taken a solemn pledge to provide service of a minimum standard and the *aam aadmi* will have a yardstick to measure the quality of this service.

Divya Bhaskar—July 10, 2006.

50 Currency Denomination Needs of the *Aam Aadmi*

Over the past five years, the Reserve Bank of India (RBI) has undertaken commendable action to ensure that the quality of currency notes has been significantly improved and that there are adequate coins of the appropriate denominations. Gone are the days when tattered notes continued in circulation and banks were callous in issuing notes of such poor quality that even the banks would not accept them back if the customer were to tender the soiled notes to the bank. Gone are the days when the general public would have fractious disputes with bus conductors and small traders would issue tokens in lieu of coins of Rs. 1 and 2 denominations. Thus, shortages of the kind experienced 10-15 years ago are no longer visible.

While every thing looks hunky-dory it is important to pick up incipient signals of impending problems.

The RBI Annual Report for 2005-06, which was released at the end of August 2006 provides a wealth of information on currency management. The Report provides data on indents and supply of notes and coins. In 2003-04 and 2004-05, the supply was close to 80 per cent of indents. Given the tendency for indents to be overestimates, supply is invariably lower than indents. In recent years, there has been a perceptible improvement in the quality of notes in circulation. The RBI has undertaken useful work to rationalise the logistics of distribution. While the Clean Note Policy and the computerisation of currency management deserve to be commended, there are a few areas which portend signs of trouble in the immediate ensuing period.

The overall supply of notes in 2005-06 was only 41 per cent of the indent as against 80 per cent in 2004-05. Even allowing for better management of movement and distribution of currency, this points to possible shortages impinging in 2006-07 and 2007-08. In the case of the Rs. 10 note, the supply in 2005-06 was only 36 per cent of the indent as against 92 per cent of the indent in 2004-05. As to a definitive answer to the question as to whether there is a shortage of the Rs. 10 note, one would need a comprehensive survey across the country. But there is a rough and ready short-cut to assess the quality of customer service. The much respected veteran commercial banker, Mr. M.G. Bhide has argued that at a first cut, one can undertake a quick assessment of the adequacy of customer service in the Fort area of Mumbai, the epicentre of the Indian financial system and if this shows inadequate service, it is a sure sign that the particular service is deficient in the rest of the country. The Bhide Rule cannot provide 100 per cent accuracy, but it serves as an reasonably accurate working rule.

The Nayak committee had, two decades ago, recommended the introduction of the Rs. 10 coin. This has been accepted by the authorities but still to be put into circulation. For a successful introduction of the Rs. 10 coin, the fresh supply of Rs. 10 notes should be drastically reduced. One hopes the authorities would move more decisively on the issue.

One needs to walk into any bank in Fort, Mumbai, and try to withdraw currency and this is what one experiences. First, the bank stocks up the Automated Teller Machines (ATMs) with high denomination notes and invariably the machine dishes out Rs. 1,000, Rs. 500 and only a few Rs. 100 notes. Secondly, in some banks, (including public sector banks) there are notices that unless one draws at least Rs. 30,000 or Rs. 15,000, across the counter service is denied. Denying a customer basic across the counter service is a violation of a bank customer's fundamental right. Thirdly, many banks are unable or unwilling to provide even a single bundle of Rs. 10 notes while new private sector banks and foreign banks do not provide a single bundle of even Rs. 20 notes. The RBI Annual Report is discreet on this issue and carefully refrains from any observation on the sharp reduction in supply of Rs. 10 notes.

Now let us turn to coins. In the Fort area of Mumbai, a large number of ATMs have been installed. Many of these machines are unable to dispense the Re. 1 and Rs. 2 coins. Currently, there appears to be sufficient Re. 1 and Rs. 2 coins in circulation, as it is easy to get back these coins in a transaction. But sooner or later, if current trends are any indication, a Re. 1 and Rs. 2 coin shortage may be lurking around the corner.

One fervently hopes that the RBI Currency Management Department and the newly set up Customer Service Department will not go into the traditional denial mode. Meanwhile, the *aam aadmi* has to suffer silently.

Divya Bhaskar—September 18, 2006.

51 Diwali Gifts for Bank Customers

Diwali is an appropriate time for stocktaking. Punters rejoice on the booming stock market, corporates gleam on their healthy bottom lines and farmers thank the heavens for good harvests. For the *aam aadmi* there is little to look forward to. This Diwali, however, bank customers have been showered with many gifts over the past few months.

The Bank Ombudsman Scheme for redressal of bank customer grievances has been revamped and hopefully there would be greater awareness of this mechanism.

The Reserve Bank of India (RBI) set up a Customer Service Department from July 1, 2006 to centralise all activity, in the RBI, relating to bank customers with a view to providing more effective implementation of these services.

The Banking Codes and Standards Board of India (BCSBI) is putting in place a mechanism for correcting systematic deficiencies in bank customer service to the *aam aadmi*. The BCSBI has set out a Code on Banks Commitment to Customers which clearly delineates the specific services a customer can expect from a bank. The Code was released on July 1, 2006 by Governor Y.V. Reddy and the RBI undertook a massive publicity campaign to make bank customers aware of their rights. Some vested interests, wishing that the BCSBI would be still-born, have spread malicious rumours and some quarters in the financial press fell for the ploy and reported that the BCSBI was not eliciting support from key banks. The canard has been laid low by the speech by Smt. K.J. Udeshi, Chairperson of the BCSBI (at the Federation of Karnataka Chambers of Commerce and Industry in Bangalore on September 11, 2006), which indicates that virtually all banks have registered with the BCSBI and all leading banks have already signed the Covenant with the BCSBI. In other words, banks are fully collaborating with the BCSBI in the effort to improve customer service.

While the Code has been adopted by most banks, it is yet to be reflected in actual implementation at the branch level. Branches of most banks in Mumbai do not have even a single copy of the Code. The BCSBI has done extremely useful work, in its short existence, but in the immediate ensuing period it needs to refocus on the task of ensuring, in a time bound manner, the availability of the Code. As a first step all banks should be required to make available for reference at each branch no later than December 31, 2006 and by the end of February 2007, (when the BCSBI completes one year of its existence), it should be ensured that each customer is given a copy. The BCSBI should quickly put in place its Field Managers who should, in the first instance, be able to give a true evaluation of adherence to a few core issues in customer service. The BCSBI should evolve a fail-safe, no fault, mechanism by which the Code can be accessed by all customers at all branches of all banks. Thereafter, the BCSBI could continue its ongoing mission of streamlining customer service. I would urge every customer to demand a copy of the Code on Banks Commitment to Customers. Customers should not hesitate to harangue bank branches, the BCSBI and the RBI for the rights promised to them.

The RBI has given a valuable Diwali gift to bank customers. On October 4, 2006, the RBI issued an important circular instruction RBI/2006-07/139 DBOD. No. Leg.BC.32/09.07.005/2006-07 on Customer Service—Non-Issuance of Passbooks to Savings Bank Accountholders (Individuals). The circular cogently argues the merits of the passbook system over the statement system. At the end of the circular the RBI says, **"Banks are therefore advised to invariably offer passbook facility to all its saving bank account holders-individuals"** (Bold letters in the circular). In case a bank offers the facility of statement of account, and the customer chooses to get statements of account, the bank must issue monthly statements of account. Effective customer service also depends on customers. Since banks have been mandated to provide passbook facilities to all savings bank account holders, customers must demand their rights and in the absence of compliance, the matter should be taken up first with the bank's own customer grievance machinery and thereafter with the Ombudsman, the BCSBI and the RBI.

The bane of the Indian financial system is excellent instructions but tardy implementation. The instruction on Savings Bank Passbook facility is a litmus test for determining whether Governor Dr. Y.V. Reddy's passion for improving bank customer service for the *aam aadmi* is going to be realised. The concerned organisations *viz.*, RBI (Customer Service Department), IBA, the Ombudsman and the BCSBI should all work in unison to ensure that the Diwali gift to the *aam aadmi* is not yet another beautifully packed gift of saw dust. There is a strong case for activism by bank customers.

Divya Bhaskar—November 6, 2006.

52 Basic Banking Facilities for the Underprivileged

India has, for years, tried to portray itself as a benevolent caring country with a strong social conscience. Our banking system, 75 per cent of which is in the public sector, prides itself for operating a myriad of special lending schemes for the weakest segments of society. Yet, the ground realities are that the Indian banking system uses differential standards of treatment. The quality of treatment depends on who you are, your standing in society and who you know. For many years I have been trying to assess banks attitude to the masses by *in cognito* visits to bank branches and I still carry the wounds inflicted on customers who are 'nobodys'. I have been shown the door after being shouted at for wanting to open a savings bank account. Now what were my shortcomings? I certainly look old—very old—I speak with a timid and hesitant voice, I wear a crumpled shirt and worn out slippers. The general run of banks feel that such a person should be turned out of the bank on grounds of KYC (Know Your Customer).

To the credit of the Reserve Bank of India (RBI) Governor, Dr. Y.V. Reddy, from the very inception of his term as Governor, he has made the provision of basic banking services to the *aam aadmi* as his cherished goal. The RBI has undertaken a series of measures to ensure that basic hassle free services are provided to all customers. There has been considerable emphasis on financial inclusion (of those kept outside the banking system because of the harsh regulations and procedures).

In these days security is of overriding priority and the fallout is that the *aam aadmi* finds it difficult to open a No Frills Savings Bank Account. Obviously, such customers are not provided cheque writing facilities so they are not potential fraudsters. But why cannot the *aam aadmi* open a Savings Bank Account? The grounds for rejection are: the person has 'No Fixed Address' established by a ration card, he owns no dwelling and cannot produce a salary slip—all good grounds for rejecting an application for opening a Savings Bank Account.

Governor Y.V. Reddy's Mid-Term Review of the Annual Policy Statement for 2006-07 is a *tour de force*, covering a gamut of complex macroeconomic and monetary developments which are naturally beyond the comprehension of the common man. The Statement, however, carries a vital paragraph (No. 127) on financial inclusion, small customers and KYC requirements. This announcement is vital as it removes the nuisance of the KYC norms for small account holders. For opening small accounts, banks need to seek only a photograph of the account holder and self-certification of address. Outstanding balances in these accounts, at any time, will be limited to Rs. 50,000 and the total transaction limit per annum would be Rs. 200,000. This is a very humane and fair measure which would take care of the problems of the deprived sectors of society which were denied the opportunity of opening a savings bank account.

We often think of the weakest segments as indolent, unreliable and spendthrift. Quite the contrary, these people invariably are hardworking, have integrity and make pathetic efforts to save small amounts. This measure is God's gift to the deprived segments of society.

Now the practice is that following the Governor's policy statement the concerned Department of the RBI issues detailed instructions to the banks. Has such a circular been issued? Bank head offices would have the excuse that they are awaiting the RBI Departmental instruction. When such an instruction is received from the RBI, the banks' head offices need to issue instructions to their branches. Now, if the head office is asked for a compliance report, they would invariably say 'Complied'. Nonetheless, the BCSBI can use the Bhide Rule that if the jargon of the banks' head offices, the word 'complied' means 'transmitted to the branches', it does not mean actually made 'operational'!

This is where the Banking Codes and Standards Board of India (BCSBI) comes in. It would be unrealistic to expect that the BCSBI should undertake a census count. If the instruction has not been put into practice in the city where the bank head office is located, it is unlikely to be effective in other branches. The BCSBI has promised to put its *in cognito* Field Officers in place. Where are they and when will they be operative? How long, oh how long, must the deprived segments wait to benefit from Governor Reddy's noble measure?

Divya Bhaskar—December 11, 2006.

53 Mumbai IFC

A Visionary Report

The Report of the High Powered Expert Committee on Making Mumbai as an International Financial Centre (Mumbai IFC), is truly a visionary document. The Report is meant for the serious minded change managers to read, reread and take studied decisions. The authors of the Report knowing the impatience of decision takers have also provided an extremely clear 21 page Executive Summary and a 24 page Summary of Recommendations. The majestic sweep of the Report is such that no one can make a claim of having fully absorbed the Report.

The Report sets out a grand vision as to how Mumbai could achieve the status of an international financial centre. In the first phase (2007-2012), Mumbai would need to connect the Indian financial system with the world's financial markets, rather like what has been done by Frankfurt, Paris, Sydney and Tokyo. In the second phase (2012-2020), Mumbai must develop the capacity to compete with the three established international financial centres *viz.*, London, New York and Singapore.

There is criticism of the Report that it does not sufficiently recognise the grassroot realities. But that is precisely what a visionary Report is meant to do if it has to stimulate the change agents into action. Visionaries are often burnt at the stakes, but out of their ashes, years later, comes belated recognition that the visionaries were saviours. Today, the Mumbai IFC Report could be buried but be sure that in 2050 policymakers would rue that had attention been given in 2007 to implementing the HPEC's Report, India would have reaped tremendous advantage. Let not our present narrow horizon prevent the authorities from carrying the ball further. The authorities need to take an early, in principle, decision on whether they see the advantages of a Mumbai IFC which has been coherently and persuasively set out in the Report. Once the authorities are convinced about the broad thrust of the proposal a High Powered

Implementation Group should be set up. This small cohesive Group should undertake ongoing work towards implementation. As such, members of the Implementation Group should be decision takers and not advisers and academics on the sidelines, who do not have any authority and therefore, no responsibility.

I would set out certain issues for discussion and the authorities response on these issues would be a gauge of the commitment of the authorities to the grand design of working towards making Mumbai as an IFC.

First, there is the issue of giving up majority public sector ownership in banks. The Narasimham Committee II (1998) had unequivocally argued that public ownership of banks and efficiency were not mutually consistent and that the majority public ownership should be given up. The 2006 Committee on Fuller Capital Account Convertibility (FCAC) reiterated the Narasimham Committee's recommendation. The HPEC has also strongly endorsed this recommendation. The banks here and now need about Rs. 45,000-50,000 crore to shore up their capital. I doubt that the government would be willing to provide this large amount without clever financial engineering. The track record in the recent period is worrisome. The takeover of RBI's stake in SBI by the government in what is called a cashless transaction, the merger of IDBI and IDBI Bank, which brings the fledgling bank back into the public sector, and the noise of the UTI Bank being brought into the public sector, are all discouraging signals, which only reinforce the government's firm commitment to continue with public ownership of banks. The HPEC unequivocally requires, as a basic prerequisite, public ownership of banks be reduced to below 49 per cent by end 2008, below 26 per cent by end 2010 and a full exit by 2015. This is a salutary recommendation, but there does not seem to be any light at the end of the tunnel.

Secondly, the HPEC argues for a rapid liberalisation of the capital account over the next 18-24 months, latest by the end of calender 2008. It bears recalling that the FCAC Committee set out a five-year roadmap ending in fiscal 2011-12. There was sharp criticism of the FCAC Report by very high decision-making levels that the Report was not ambitious enough. But there are no signs that the authorities intend to step up the implementation in a shorter timeframe.

There are a number of vital issues on which the HPEC has made recommendations, *inter alia* including autonomy of the RBI, separation of debt management and monetary policy and a wide gamut of measures on market development. This short column cannot make a pretence of having toughed the fringe of the HPEC recommendations. The HPEC Report deserves serious examination by parliamentarians, policymakers, civil servants, financial sector honchos, academics and the discerning public at large.

The nation owes a debt to the HPEC, as also its erstwhile Chairman, Mr. Percy Mistry; the Report bears the unmistakable imprimatur of Mr. Percy Mistry, and whatever view one may take on the internal tensions in the Committee, it does not detract from the high quality of the Report.

54 The *Aam Aadmi* Assesses Bank's Customer Service in Ahmedabad

At one end of the spectrum we are assured that the soporific Indian banking system has the best technology in the world. We are on the cusp of a major breakthrough in providing quality banking services. At the other end of the spectrum, the *aam aadmi* struggles to obtain basic simple banking services. When these issues are brought into the open, the blame game starts. The Reserve Bank of India (RBI) fumes that the banks are not following the regulatory instructions. The banks, in turn, claim that all the woes of the *aam aadmi* lie in the regulatory framework. The Office of the Banking Ombudsman tries to alleviate the customer problems in individual cases, while the Banking Codes and Standards Board of India (BCSBI) attempts to rectify systemic deficiencies. The Indian Banks' Association (IBA) has queered the pitch by asserting that "lack of appreciation on the part of the BCSBI in considering practical issues in implementing ... the banks were in a position to fully fund BCSBI and should take over this responsibility from RBI" (*IBA Newsletter*, May 2007, Page 3). Some bright spark may persuade the IBA to say that it can afford to finance RBI's regulatory/supervisory activities and is, therefore, ready to take over the RBI functions. The RBI has to intervene quickly to restore sanity and instill mutual respect among all concerned institutions.

What is happening at the grassroots level? The present columnist attempted a three day *in cognito* visit of banks in Ahmedabad (public, private, foreign and urban cooperative). The Survey was by no means comprehensive and covered only eight banks which have a predominant presence in Gujarat. In fact, the endeavour was limited to assessing very simple services sought by depositors.

The one thing which is gratifying is that there was a pervasive sense of politeness, reflective perhaps of the culture of Ahmedabad.

Banks are required to have a "Help You Desk". Only one public sector bank had a proper functioning "Help You Desk". Two public sector banks with a strong presence in Gujarat did not have any functioning "Help You Desks". In fact, in one public sector bank the desk was occupied by three helmets! In one of these public sector banks, the Deputy General Manager, on seeing a confused client invited our *aam aadmi* to his cabin and explained the procedures for opening an account.

On the procedure for opening a Savings Bank Account, a problem faced was that after producing all identification *viz.*, PAN card, voter card, electricity/telephone bill, the public sector banks and urban cooperative bank insisted on a letter of introduction from an existing customer of their bank. In the case of one public sector bank, the bank was willing to accept a signature verification from the existing banker. In one of the aggressive new private sector banks, seeing a senior citizen, the bank tried to inveigle the customer with all kinds of sops but at each stage the minimum balance was raised. In one foreign bank, the bank was satisfied with standard identification and no introduction was required from an existing customer of the bank. It is unfortunate that in none of the banks the Savings Bank Rules were available. Banks were unanimously of the view that the insistence on an introduction from an existing customer of the bank was attributed to the Know Your Customer (KYC) norms set out by the RBI.

On the issue of death of a depositor, one public sector bank, one urban cooperative bank and one foreign bank had a clear understanding of the RBI's revised guidelines under which the banks would be undertaking a satisfactory discharge if the survivors/nominees in the bank account were given the balance in the deceased's account. In contrast three private sector banks and two public sector banks were unsure as to how to handle the account of the deceased depositor and were unaware about the simplified procedures and were still in the mode of determining legal heirs.

As regards the role of the Ombudsman, two public sector banks and one foreign bank were aware of the correct procedures and had clearly visible notice boards on the Ombudsman, while one public sector bank, one cooperative bank and three private sector banks had incorrect information or were blissfully unaware of the role of the Ombudsman.

As regards the existence of the Code on Banks' Commitment to Customers, only one public sector bank was aware of the Code but was not distributing the Code to customers. Two public sector banks, three private sector banks and one foreign bank were totally oblivious of the Code.

While one should refrain from generalisations, it would appear that bank customers are not aware of their rights and the communications from banks head offices to the branches is very poor. The journey forward is long and arduous but the RBI, the IBA, the banks and BCSBI need to work in concert with mutual respect. All economic agents have to imbibe the simple dictum set out by the Chairman BCSBI, Smt. Kishore Udeshi: "Without depositors there would be no banks".

Divya Bhaskar—May 28, 2007.

55 India's Homegrown Sub-prime Credit Crisis

The international economy has been rocked, in recent months, by the so called 'Sub-prime Credit Crisis'. The question that is uppermost is whether the international economy is on the verge of a deep recession. The US Fed, the European Central Bank and the Bank of England have attempted to shore up confidence by readily providing large liquidity support.

The question being asked is what would be the impact on India? Will the weak dollar stimulate capital inflows into the emerging economies? *Per contra*, will investors pull back their funds from emerging markets to shore up their positions in their own home countries? The Reserve Bank of India, the Prime Minister's Economic Advisory Council and the Ministry of Finance would no doubt carefully prepare for any eventualities.

But there is another sinister nemesis lurking round the corner in India, *viz.*, the homegrown sub-prime lending. After four years of unabated credit expansion with phenomenally high expansion for personal loans, credit cards, real estate, housing and capital market activity, doubts are being expressed about the safety of such credit. Banks have been, rather naively shouting, from the rooftops, that such loans are totally safe. As the overall credit expansion was unusually high the fall in Non-Performing Assets (NPAs) has to some extent been a statistical phenomenon.

It appears that the music has stopped. Banks which dealt with recovery with insouciance are now going to the other extreme of using musclemen to recover loans. While there is no hard data on bank lapses in securing adequate collateral, there is anecdotal evidence that in some cases banks have given more than the value of the security and what is even worse is that in some cases there is no collateral at all in housing loans.

In the area of personal loans, banks have felt that this is the safest business as borrowers have high income and even though there is no collateral there is no fear of NPAs. New private sector banks and foreign banks went into overdrive and public sector banks, not to be left behind, jumped into the fray. Till a few months ago, a premier bank of the country carried a prime time TV advertisement that not only does the bank give you a loan to cover the cost of the housing but house improvement loans and even gives an add on for the borrower to splurge on his marriage. Note that such exuberance has now disappeared from the advertisements. The RBI has, for quite some time, expressed concern about such lending but bank helmsmen have not cared to heed the sagacious advice.

Then there are credit card risks which all know emanate from reckless foisting of credit cards on passive customers, who do not even seek these facilities. In the quest to show that small boys are now the tallest men, some banks have gone on an aggressive expansion of these facilities. Banks are attracted to this business as hidden charges result in high effective interest rates on such facilities, without an understanding of adverse selection, resulting in an increase in the riskiest lending. There is no better way of picking up NPAs!

I have been favoured access to some back of envelope calculations undertaken by Shri M.G. Bhide, one of India's most versatile and cerebral bankers, on sub-prime lending relating to credit cards and personal loans (other than three wheeler finance). While Shri Bhide is by no means answerable for these calculations, surely bankers with their large resources of manpower should be able to undertake honest calculations of the homegrown sub-prime lending. Personal Loan Pools securitised by Credit Rating Agencies during the past 12 months are estimated at Rs. 4,800 crore while other Personal Loan Pools are estimated at Rs. 2000 crore. Personal Loans outstanding on the books of banks and non-bank financial companies are estimated at Rs. 35,000 crore and about 80 per cent or Rs. 28,000 crore are sub-prime. The credit card dues outstanding are estimated at Rs. 16,000 crore and an estimated 40 per cent are hard core roll overs which can be considered to be sub-prime. In effect these two categories have a staggering Rs. 41,200 of sub-prime lending which could explode at any moment. There are very large tracts of sub-prime lending in other sectors. The large incremental lending of the past four years has created a false sense of euphoria that we have licked the NPA problem and our profit lines are healthy and we are ready to deal with international competition in 2009. Banks should shed their bravado and, instead of getting into an aggressive denial of the Bhide exercise, should undertake a serious introspection. Rather than bad mouthing these back of envelope calculations, the IBA, the banks, the Raghuram Rajan Committee and the RBI should undertake a serious exercise to access these problems and work towards mitigation of losses. Loosening monetary policy to resolve these problems by lowering policy signalling interest rates or lowering reserve requirements would be an inappropriate response.

Divya Bhaskar—October 1, 2007.

56 Financial Regulation and Supervision

Need for a Killer Instinct

Financial liberalisation has been the focus of a number of Committee Reports in India over the past two decades. Unfortunately, the need for change in financial regulation and supervision has not attracted adequate and meaningful debate. Much of the debate has been on whether this activity should be taken out from the Reserve Bank of India (RBI). Advocates see merit in setting up a dedicated Financial Oversight Authority as a panacea for the problems of the Indian financial system. International experience is equivocal in that some see the UK Financial Services Authority (FSA) as the ultimate model to follow while others point to the system where there are advantages in the central bank undertakes this activity, especially as the central bank is the ultimate authority for providing liquidity. The jury is still out on this issue.

The debate in India has been on whether there should be a single regulator/supervisor for the entire financial system or there should be multiple authorities. In some ways the debate in India has developed in a tangential manner. There is too much debate on who should regulate/supervise and little or no debate on how to regulate/supervise. In recent years RBI and SEBI have been undertaking heroic efforts to get rid of the shackles of the complex and unnecessary minutiae of regulation. The regulatory framework is still convoluted but so is it in most advanced financial markets. The central issue was pithily summed up by John Crow, Governor of the Bank of Canada in the mid-1990s, in his C.D. Deshmukh Memorial Lecture, wherein he cautioned that "deregulation does not mean desupervision." In fact, deregulation requires a more active supervisory process.

There is a need to focus greater attention on how supervision is undertaken. Supervision is a very specialised skill and a generalist cannot be expected to undertake this activity—it is rather like a general physician undertaking complicated neuro-surgery.

Both RBI and SEBI (and for that matter other regulators like the insurance and pensions authorities) need to develop Multi-Disciplinary Supervisory Strike Forces which undertake effective supervision with lightening speed. This has two problems. First, the remuneration package in RBI and SEBI does not attract the most competent talent. Secondly, skilled chartered accountants, lawyers and financial analysts would not dedicate their entire services to the supervisory authorities. Supervisors would, therefore, need to employ such skilled personnel for specific projects for short periods and remunerate them adequately. This is easier said than done. It is difficult to administer a Supervisory Strike Force wherein the Head gets the remuneration of a *Babu* while his subordinate gets a fat cat remuneration. Nonetheless, it is imperative that these issues be addressed expeditiously.

The bane of financial supervision, in the Indian context, is the attitude towards supervision. In the heydays of the dirigiste regime the best performers sought out and got the plus posts in Regulation and the poorer performers were relegated to Supervision. This was poignantly brought out in the mid-1990s when one of India's most competent bankers was appointed as Deputy Governor but a few days before taking charge he was told that he would be Deputy Governor in charge of Supervision, to which he quickly declined the offer. Such an attitude was not always so. In the pre-nationalisation period, it was the most competent officers who undertook supervision and the leader of the supervisory team felt that he occupied the pride of place.

If supervision is to be effective there has to be a change in the mindset. The Supervisor has to ensure that any wrong doing by a bank or institution invites peremptory penalties and there should be no weakening of the supervisors resolve to impose punishment. Why do banks strictly adhere to the cash reserve ratio and the statutory liquidity ratio? The answer is that in 1981-82 when there were endemic defaults as also in 1990-1992 when the defaults were connected to the securities scandal, the RBI stood firm on penalties. In the Indian firmament there is an almost universal attitude that "*Bechara phas gaya, jane do* (the poor fellow got caught, let him go)." If supervision is to be effective one has to get out of the compassionate approach and supervisors have to develop a killer approach.

Divya Bhaskar—May 26, 2008.

VI

57 The Sad Saga of NRO Accounts

The origin of the Non-Resident Ordinary (NRO) Accounts in banks relates to the days when there was an acute shortage of foreign exchange. Indian residents abroad were required to convert their resident rupee account to a Non-Resident Ordinary (NRO) Account. These funds were non-repatriable both for capital as well as income. Non-residents could only use these funds for use in India and were allowed to pay for their air tickets.

With the advent of current account convertibility, the investment income accruing to NRO Accounts was allowed to be repatriated but subject to rather complex procedures and it was necessary to produce a Chartered Accountant's Certificate even in cases where the income tax assessment was completed and invariably a refund was given to the tax payer.

With the gradual liberalisation of the capital account, the limit for annual remittance was gradually raised and by 2003 NRO Account holders were allowed to repatriate US$ one million per annum. Paradoxically, along with the liberalisation of NRO Accounts, remittances and procedures were tightened even for small amounts.

Some illustrations would enable one to get an idea of how insensate the system has become. Since the account carried a clause that the funds were "non-repatriable", shares held by the non-resident were also labelled as "non-repatriable" notwithstanding the fact that NRO Account holders were permitted to remit abroad up to US$ one million, including inheritances.

Residents can remit out of the country up to US$ 200,000 per annum with relatively easy procedures. Moreover, for all remittances up to US$ 5,000, the A2 Form was dispensed with, but the banks with their visceral memories of being severely penalised for the absence of the A2 form, continue to call for the A2 Form. In 2004, the requirement that the remitter was required to make the obnoxious declaration of what he was not doing by way of contravention of the Foreign Exchange Management Act (FEMA) was altered to a simple declaration of what the remitter was doing. The ground reality in the year 2008 is that in some banks the NRO Account holders are required to fill both the new declaration as also the old declaration. Irrespective of the amount the remitter has to fill the A2 Form and also obtain a Chartered Accountant's Certificate.

Some banks, in their role as depositary participants (DPs), claim that NRO Account holders who inherit shares in a Demat account have to comply with EC Co. FT 1/434/11.01.010 (17) 2001-02 dated August 17, 2001 where there is a reference to the Portfolio Investment Scheme (PIS). Some banks insist that NRO Account holders, who wish to deal in the secondary market, are required to obtain permission for PIS and follow the RBI guidelines. The NRO Account holder is required to make a declaration that he/she will not transact in the secondary market unless they obtain specific permission in writing by submitting an application for PIS as per RBI guidelines. NRO Account holders cannot receive inherited shares into their Demat account without the permission of the DP and should have a PIS.

Furthermore some banks indicate that they will apply a 30 per cent tax deduction at source (TDS) on the analogy of TDS on interest income from fixed deposits and Savings Bank Accounts. Is there a mix up of an asset with an income? Under the provisions of Section 195, when a resident enters into a buying transaction with a non-resident, the resident is required to impose a 30 per cent TDS on the proceeds paid to the non-resident and it is for the non-resident to seek a refund from the tax authorities. How does a resident comply with the provisions of Section 195 when there is anonymous screen-based trading? In any case, the bank is not the buyer and there is no need for the bank to be overzealous to undertake a TDS on an asset sale to which the bank is not a party.

Thus, NRO Account holders need to be treated with transparent, simple rules and guidelines. Once NRO Accounts have become repatriable up to US$ one million per annum, the whole set of rules and regulations need to be revamped. Surely RBI/SEBI and others concerned can alleviate the suffering of NRO Account holders.

As Ms. K.J. Udeshi, Chairman, Banking Codes and Standards Board of India, aptly put it, by delegating powers to banks, we have moved from a single regulator (RBI) to multiple regulators (banks), each of whom have their own interpretation. What is needed is not more capital liberalisation but removal of the knots which are a relic of the past. It is not enough for the regulator to understand the extant instructions; it is more important that the banks and users (NRO Account holders) understand. The intent of policy should be reflected in the content of policy and the content of policy should be reflected in actual operations.

Divya Bhaskar—July 21, 2008.

58 Fuller Capital Account Convertibility and Everyday Life

In recent months, there has been a raging public debate on what is called "Fuller Capital Account Convertibility". One would have thought that this abstruse subject would be of interest only to the specialists in finance, corporates and banks. On the contrary no subject fires up the minds of the general public as the issue of convertibility. What is so magical about this issue that drives people's interest?

To get an understanding of the issue we need to go back to the start of World War II. During the War, foreign exchange became a scarce commodity, and countries, including India, introduced draconian exchange controls. In India, exchange controls became progressively stringent from the 1950s. The *aam aadmi* was frightened of the exchange controls and there was fear of punitive punishment for relatively minor and frivolous violations. I recall that shortly after I joined the Reserve Bank of India in the early 1960s a visibly shaken old man came to me for help. His problem was that he had inherited, from his uncle in the UK, a few shares in a dormant tea company. The share was quoted at two farthings. Today's reader is not expected to know what a "farthing" meant. In those days the British pound had 20 shillings and each shilling had 12 pence and each penny had four farthings. The sterling-rupee rate was quoted at one shilling six pence to the rupee. Now the total shares held by the old man would be less than one rupee. A senior officer of the RBI told me rather sternly that the old man had violated the foreign exchange regulations and that he could be put behind bars for a minimum period of six months. He was, however, kind enough to say that even though the violation could not be ignored, he promised to look into the matter. The diligent officer put up a long note to the Department Head with the recommendation that the punishment be waived. The old man was forever grateful for escaping the harsh penalty!

Matters were gradually streamlined but foreign exchange remained a scarce commodity till the early 1990s. The forbidden fruit (foreign exchange) was much sought after and a rich uncle from the United States who gave you a couple of dollars was your favourite relative.

All this changed in the 1990s. First, by 1994, current account transactions were freed and the draconian act was diluted. From 1997 a gradual process of liberalisation of the capital account was initiated. Put simply, capital account convertibility refers to the freedom to convert local financial assets into foreign financial assets and vice versa. While capital controls were for corporates, banks and non-bank institutions were relaxed, the harsh controls remained for individuals. Resident individuals were considered as *chors* (thieves) and if they were provided any element of capital account convertibility, resident individuals would run away with the entire money supply of the country! This was a totally erroneous perception. The forbidden fruit, which is freely available, is no longer cherished. From February 2004 residents were allowed to take out US$ 25,000 per year and can open foreign currency accounts abroad; yet very little has gone out.

With the great Indian diaspora, every Pappu and his uncle has a non-resident relative. This is not restricted to high-tech professionals but small traders, tailors, carpenters, plumbers, electricians, cobblers, maids and what have you. Non-resident Indians are now allowed to take out US$ one million per annum from their non-resident ordinary accounts which till recently were non-repatriable.

The Report on Fuller Capital Account Convertibility (July 2006) recommended that there should be a gradual liberalisation over a period of five years. The Report, however, stressed that the timing and sequencing of measures of capital liberalisation should be dependent on what are called the accompanying "concomitants" i.e., fiscal consolidation, strengthening of the banking system, development of financial markets and effective and consistent monetary and exchange rate policies. As there is progress on the concomitants, there could be progressive liberalisation of capital controls.

What should be of interest to the general public is that resident individuals should be provided progressively higher limits for capital account remittances. In a significant move, the RBI announced on October 31, 2006 that individual residents can remit on current and capital account US $ 50,000 per financial year as against US $ 25,000 hithereto (subsequently this was raised, in stages to US $ 200,000 per annum). This is a significant measure. Allowing this limit for remittances by resident individuals more than meets the criteria of reasonableness and it can truly be said that the *aam aadmi*, for all practical purposes, now enjoys "Fuller Capital Account Convertibility". We are no longer dependent on our rich uncle from America for a few dollars. The state has been reached where we are dollar rich but rupee poor (in other words we do not have enough rupees to buy the dollars permitted)—this is the true meaning of convertibility!

Divya Bhaskar—December 4, 2006.

59 Use Forex Reserves Without Violating RBI's Balance Sheet

The use of the foreign exchange reserves of the Reserve Bank of India (RBI) for developing the infrastructure has been a favourite hobby horse of the Government of India for the past three decades. As far back as 1977-78, when H.M. Patel was the Finance Minister, the Union Budget came up with a presentation of the budget deficit of something like Rs. 800 crore and with use of forex reserves the deficit was shown as Rs. 500 crore; fortunately, the idea was abandoned. Again, in 1995-96, the Planning Commission raised the issue of the use of RBI's forex reserves, but the snag was that the RBI would need to provide the rupees with which the RBI's forex reserves would be bought; the RBI and the Ministry of Finance did not agree and the proposal was aborted. During the past two years, the proposal has, once again, been revived and this time round the government has set up a Committee under Shri Deepak Parekh, Chairman HDFC, to work out the modalities of stepping up investments in the infrastructure. It appears that the game plan is to set up a Special Purpose Vehicle (SPV) which will invest the reserves in high yielding assets and provide support to infrastructure projects.

Before going into the merits of the proposal, a few principles need to be enunciated. First, if India wishes to step up the investment rate, given the savings rate, the gap between savings and investment should be increased. The obverse of this is that the current account deficit (CAD) in the balance of payments has to be widened from the present rate of 1.5-2.0 per cent to say 4.0 per cent of GDP. If this happens be sure that the rating agencies will put out warning signals and foreign investors would flee.

Let us assume that the government decides to run a large CAD. If the SPV wishes to buy say US $ 10 billion, the snag is that someone has to down the rupees to enable RBI to part with its reserves. It is here that the issue of the integrity of the RBI balance sheet comes to the fore. It is important to protect the sanctity of the RBI balance sheet. The RBI just cannot be expected to provide both the forex reserves as well as the rupee resources; if the RBI were to do so there would be a gaping hole in the RBI balance sheet. The government would not wish to down the rupees because of the Fiscal Responsibility and Budget Management (FRBM) commitments. When the SPV acquires reserves it has no rupees to pay for the forex purchases so the fledgling organisation will try to push SPV Bonds down the throat of the RBI. The RBI auditors surely cannot accept the weakling SPV Bonds as standard assets and would require the RBI to make provisions for such dubious assets. The RBI should never accept SPV Bonds, with or without, government guarantee.

Another idea is that the forex reserves of the RBI should be placed with the Asian Development Bank (ADB). How would the ADB pay rupees to the RBI? The ADB raises bonds in the rupee market, and the ADB would swap the rupees for RBI's reserves, and in turn lend the forex to the infrastructure projects. The ADB should lend the rupees to the Indian projects and each project could use the rupees to buy forex from the Indian market. If this could be done, why should the RBI place its forex reserves with the ADB? If all this is to earn a higher rate of return on the forex reserves, someone has to bear the risks. The short answer is that the Indian infrastructure projects would bear the risk in terms of a higher interest rate. We would no doubt be told that some other country, say the mythical country of Mancunia, has done an SPV and we should follow suit.

It has been also argued that the rate of return on the reserves is low and needs to be raised. Central banks are rightly cautious in the deployment of reserves. If the government wishes to be daring, it should, in writing, confirm that the RBI should invest a specified portion of the reserves in investments like Triple A Bonds, equity, real estate and gold. Given counter-cyclical movements in currency and gold prices, diversifying a portion of reserves into gold makes eminent sense. But government should transparently endorse the quest for higher returns. In the absence of such a commitment, in the event of adverse developments, the RBI will unfairly be burnt at the stakes.

The Deepak Parekh Committee has a difficult task of finding a viable solution. History provides a possible solution. In the 1950s India had huge sterling balances and as a conscious policy, in the Second Five Year Plan, these balances were run down to finance the setting up of major steel plants at Bhilai, Durgapur and Rourkela. In today's context, infrastructure projects may need subventions, but subventions should be the exclusive prerogative of the government. Plundering the RBI's balance sheet is something no government should consider.

Divya Bhaskar—February 5, 2007.

60 Appreciation of the Rupee

Playing with Fire

In recent months, the Indian rupee has appreciated in relation to other major currencies, particularly the US dollar. What does the exchange rate signify? In layman's language, it is the number of rupees one has to offer to buy one unit of foreign exchange. Till recently, the exchange rate was US \$ 1=Rs. 45 and advocates of appreciation are ecstatic that the rate is now close to US \$ 1=Rs. 40.

To the extent we manage some sort of market related exchange rate, of course, with periodic intervention by the Reserve Bank of India (RBI), there must be some underlying rationale for the exchange rate. Although we do not follow a US \$-rupee peg, the public perception of an appreciation or depreciation is always considered in relation to the US dollar. Most economists, central bankers, commercial bankers, government policymakers and other policy opinion makers, cannot instantly tell us the rate of the rupee in relation to the Euro, the Yen or Sterling. For the *Pundits* what used to be relevant, some years ago, was the real effective exchange rate (REER) (which is nothing more than a composite trade weighted exchange rate index with a neutral base date of 1993-94 adjusted for inflation rate differentials). Until 1997, the RBI and the government swore by the REER as the Pole Star guiding exchange rate policy. In the post-1997 period, the RBI de-emphasised the REER in its official pronouncements on the ground that the neutral REER would vary depending on which year was taken as the base. Nonetheless, analysts observed that the rupee, in practice, generally moved in a narrow range of + or – 5 per cent of the neutral REER base for 1993-94. In the post-2003 period, REER was partially restored to the pre-1997 deity status.

Exchange rate management has become complex in recent years with the conflict of managing the exchange rate along with a liberalised capital account and an independent monetary policy. While, till recently, the RBI has been intervening in the forex market buying dollars, the resultant release of domestic liquidity has required the authorities to issue bonds under the Market Stabilisation Scheme (MSS), absorb liquidity under the Liquidity Adjustment Facility (LAF) through the reverse repo facility (surplus liquidity in the market is placed with the RBI at a rate of interest of 6 per cent) and the cash reserve ratio (CRR). All this sterilisation has costs but, these measures increased interest rates in India and stimulated even larger capital flows.

In recent months there has been an overriding preoccupation, quite correctly, with controlling inflation as the over 6 per cent inflation rate was not acceptable. The authorities changed tracks and there was, for a while, a cessation of RBI intervention in the forex market and the rupee appreciated to around US $ 1=Rs. 40.50. The advocates of appreciation see this as a tool for lowering the inflation. It is persuasively argued that the appreciation would reduce import costs and thereby curb inflation. What is more, the International Monetary Fund has blessed the appreciation. In an article in the Indian Press by two IMF economists, Kalpana Kochhar and Charles Kramer (*Business Standard,* May 12, 2007) advocate appreciation of the rupee on the ground that it reduces inflation. Somewhat surprising is the assertion that a strong rupee does not reduce the rupee value of export earnings. India is not an international price maker but a price taker and it is simplistic to say that the Indian exporter will not suffer. It is surprising that the learned IMF economists argue against fundamentals. With an appreciation the present current account deficit in the balance of payments would eventually rise to unsustainable levels and sooner or later foreign investors would flee from India.

Elementary economics would point to the fact that a depreciation, through absorption of liquidity, eventually reduces inflation and a country with higher inflation relative to the rest of the world, which undertakes appreciation, worsens its problems. The government and RBI should listen to stalwarts like Shankar Acharya, A.V. Rajwade and Ajit Ranade who all warn about the dangers of appreciation.

The Indian authorities should simply get back to forex intervention and sterilisation through the MSS, the LAF and CRR. The costs of sterilisation are far less than the damage of appreciation of the rupee. Furthermore, the RBI and government should remove the froth from capital flows. We must have faith in ourselves. Let us not believe that stopping Participatory Notes (PNs), which is a euphemism for illicit activity, will change the sentiment of genuine foreign investors. Furthermore, the authorities should simply close the Foreign Currency Non-Resident Banks Scheme (FCNRB) as this deposit facility for non-resident Indians has no place in today's milieu.

The present policy of appreciation of the rupee is fundamentally flawed and the authorities are playing with fire.

Divya Bhaskar—June 11, 2007.

61 Infrastructure Financing and RBI Reserves

In the past two years, there has been discussion on using India's forex reserves for development of the infrastructure. Using forex reserves to meet the foreign exchange component of infrastructure projects is not the problem. The real problem is the development of viable infrastructure projects and garnering of rupee resources. The RBI forex reserves should be used transparently without violating the integrity of the RBI balance sheet. It is from this standpoint that the entire focus in the recent period on forex reserves has been a false start.

As far back as the 1950s India drew down its forex reserves to meet the forex component of the three steel plants—Durgapur, Rourkela and Bhilai. The government laid down the rupees to buy the forex reserves from the RBI and consequently the budget deficit was higher.

In 1978 there was an upsurge of forex reserves and the government showed a smaller deficit by indicating the use of forex reserves. In the political turmoil of 1978-79 this false start was given a quiet burial.

The idea of using the forex reserves for infrastructure financing was revived in 1995-96 by the Planning Commission. By then the concept of the gross fiscal deficit had been established and the government did not want to show a higher deficit and hence what was mooted was that the RBI's forex reserves would be drawn down without the government laying down the rupees. This proposal was firmly rejected by both the RBI and the Ministry of Finance.

At the present time, with the Fiscal Responsibility and Budget Management Act in place the government is keen to use the forex reserves without impacting on the gross fiscal deficit.

India's infrastructure financing requirements for the next five years are estimated at US $ 475 billion, but the bulk of this would be a rupee requirement. The crucial problem is that the government just does not have the wherewithal to raise the rupee resources. What the government is doing is to wish away the problem by envisaging that the Special Purpose Vehicle (SPV) would borrow the forex reserves from the RBI.

The recent proposal is that the newly set up India Infrastructure Finance Company (IIFC) would borrow US $ 10 billion from the RBI. Of this amount US $ 5 billion would be used as a "credit wrap" which would be an insurance cover for the IIFC to raise more funds abroad. This proposal has been shot down by the RBI as it would violate the RBI Act.

As regards the balance US $ 5 billion the IIFC would invest it abroad so as to earn a return higher than what the RBI does. How has the IIFC acquired such skills? The cat comes out of the bag! The IIFC would pass on these funds to some other agency abroad which would invest these funds in assets the RBI cannot invest in. This is a violation of the RBI Act, at least in spirit. Legal experts need to see if this can be challenged in the courts. Can Parliament and the RBI auditors be silent spectators while all this is going on. If the government wants the reserves to earn a higher return, with the attendant risks, it should seek an amendment of the law. This is a cloak and dagger operation to provide some income to the IIFC which would otherwise find it difficult to earn its keep. I see no merit in this proposal. The argument that Ruritania or Mancunia have done so is no reason for India to follow suit.

Development finance institutions have no role in a system in which we are not willing to dole out funds for concessional raising of funds and allowing below cost lending. The setting up of the IIFC is a false start. So also the Infrastructure Development Finance Company (IDFC), though to its credit it has restructured its activities to rebalance its portfolio so as to be viable.

The right approach would have been to create a giant consortium of SBI, ICICI, IDBI, IIFC, IDFC ILFS, EXIM and large public, private and foreign banks which would then be able to rise the large rupee resources required for infrastructure. The government cannot renege its responsibility for financing infrastructure. The government has to choose how it deploys its resources. What is important today? Holding on the yesteryear's philosophy of majority ownership of banks or rapidly developing the infrastructure. We are at the crossroads of the life of the nation. If the government gradually off-loads its majority stake in public sector banks it will be able to find the rupees for infrastructure development. The forex reserves use issue is a red herring. If those financing the infrastructure produce the rupees, the RBI would gladly provide the forex funds. There is no dearth of forex reserves. We need sensible decisions on finding the rupees. The infrastructure can never be developed by pilfering the RBI forex reserves by US $ 10 billion. Why do we need to undertake imprudent policies when we are on the cusp of becoming a world leader?

Divya Bhaskar—July 23, 2007.

62 Preparing for Large Two-Way Capital Flows

The turmoil in recent weeks in major international financial markets ought to have a sobering effect on us in India. We have a characteristic tendency for one way movements. We feel that we are invincible and will always remain the country of the hour; that foreign investors will continue to invest in India irrespective of what happens in global financial markets and irrespective of what happens in the political economy of India. While there is a need for realistic preparation for extremely high volatility in capital flows, there is a strong viewpoint that such thoughts are alarmistic and are labelled as self-fulfilling prophecies. We are thus, strongly advised to be positive and to think out of the box and make ourselves believe that all is well on the capital flows front. The harsh reality is that we could face a difficult two-way situation, both of which are not easily predictable.

Much to the chagrin of the optimists who see "all clear" signals, I would dare to portend that India should be ready, over the next three months, for a pouring in of say US $ 50 billion into the forex reserves and *per contra*, be also ready for a capital outflow of say US $ 50 billion in a three month period. It could well be that neither of this takes place and that the Indian ship sails in calm waters. It is, however, better to be safe and prepare for the worst rather than be sorry after the event.

Let us take the first possibility that US $ 50 billion pours into the Indian reserves as investors exit from the US dollar. In such an event we should, in preparation, quickly squeeze out the present excess liquidity by the RBI reverse repo operations as also the Market Stabilisation Scheme (MSS) and the cash reserve ratio (CRR) so as to ensure that excess liquidity does not slosh around. In any case we should not countenance any further appreciation of the rupee. If large liquidity is left unsterilised it will sooner or later show up in monetary expansion and inflation, hurting the common person.

Now, if US $ 50 billion exits from India, what should we do? One view is that as domestic liquidity shrinks all that the authorities need to do is to replace the liquidity by RBI injecting funds into the system and all would be well. Replacing liquidity when there is a haemorrhage of forex reserves will only generate further loss of forex reserves. In this situation the authorities should let the excess liquidity work itself off and at best there should be only smoothening operations to ensure that there is an orderly contraction of liquidity. In any case the authorities should never fully counter the liquidity contraction. The exchange rate appreciation of the early months of 2007 should be clawed back and the rupee should be allowed to depreciate in an orderly manner. There would be a clamour for a reduction in the CRR and a lowering of the policy interest rate on the repo (under which the RBI injects liquidity). The reduction in the CRR and the policy rate should be grudgingly slow and substantially lagged over market expectations. In fact, the ideal would be an increase in the CRR and interest rates. It is doubtful if the RBI would be able to undertake such harsh measures and would do well not to loosen monetary policy when forex reserves decline. Beyond a point, if forex reserve losses continue, harsh monetary measures become unavoidable.

The past three years have witnessed very large credit expansion and the slowing down of credit expansion in recent months should not be reversed by policy measures. Advocates of replacing domestic liquidity contraction would make shrill noises about the adverse impact on growth and employment. The RBI must resist such pleas and not back off from its present stance. Yielding to such pleas would be a sure way of ensuring that inflation veers towards double digits.

The formulation and implementation of monetary policy is already more difficult than it has ever been. It would be of little solace to the RBI if one were to portend that these difficulties are going to rise manifold in the months to come, irrespective of whichever way capital flows move. Whoever said that the lives of central bankers would ever be easy!

Divya Bhaskar—September 3, 2007.

63 Dealing with the Capital Inflow Tsunami

The Reserve Bank of India (RBI) forex reserves have increased by about US $ 50 billion in the current financial year. The Sensex is in close range of 18,000, though it could crash any moment. Do we rejoice and celebrate that we have never had it so good and that we are the champions in the international economic league? The capital inflows Tsunami would be of concern to the monetary policymakers in the temple of money.

The institutions which undertake forecasts seem to veer around to a real growth of the economy of around 8.5 per cent in 2007-08. With the favourable monsoon, agricultural output should be good and with robust growth in services and a modest growth in industry, the overall growth of the economy in 2007-08 should top 9 per cent. The inflation rate, on a year-on-year basis is currently around 3.5 per cent but, in a few months, the inflation rate could accelerate to well over 5 per cent and if international oil and other vital commodity prices remain firm, the inflation rate could top 6 per cent by the end of March 2008.

How should the RBI react in terms of its monetary policy in the second half of 2007-08? The one thing that stands out is the continuing appreciation of the rupee. Macho spirits are talking about the rupee rising to US $ 1=Rs. 37, but this would be sheer *hara-kiri*. Our inflation rate is clearly higher than that of the major industrial countries and we have a continuing balance of payments current account deficit. Riding the crest of the capital inflows would be dangerous and sooner or later the country will have to pay the price for foolhardy policies.

The RBI has been fighting a heroic battle to contain the appreciation of the rupee. The government has already had to provide large sops to the export sector and the uncompetitiveness would show up in other sectors. While the doves would argue that we should reduce reserve requirements and interest rates, the need of the hour is clearly strong monetary policy action.

Money supply (M3) is growing at an unacceptable annual rate of 20 per cent while reserve money (the money created by the RBI) is growing at an even higher annual rate of 25 per cent. Inflation looms round the corner like a sinister nemesis.

The choices are clear: Either the authorities curb the capital inflows (which they are not willing to do) or they should bear the cost of sterilisation of excessive capital flows. The third option of appreciating the rupee is so disastrous that it should be totally ruled out. What is outlined below is a strategy for dealing with the capital inflows.

The first measure has been already announced *viz.*, the enhancement of the Market Stabilisation Scheme ceiling from Rs. 150,000 crore to Rs. 200,000 crore. At the ceiling, the cost to the government would be Rs. 14,000 crore per annum. It would not be reasonable to expect the government to further increase this limit during the rest of the current financial year. The unutilised limit should be used selectively and a part of the fire power should be kept in readiness when there is a further onslaught of capital inflows.

When capital inflows are large, banks deposits increase effortlessly and as such it is only fair to expect banks to participate in the burden sharing of the cost of sterilisation. The present excess liquidity in the system is very high and accordingly the cash reserve ratio (CRR) should be raised in November 2007 by one percentage point, which would immobilise about Rs. 28,000 crore.

From December 2007, the RBI should switch over to a 10 per cent incremental cash reserve ratio. The advantage of this measure is that there is an automatic immobilising of excess liquidity, without the tensions of policy tightening.

The RBI should refrain for being persuaded by pleas that interest should be paid on CRR balances as this attenuates the efficacy of this instrument.

As a rule of thumb, if absorption of liquidity under the reverse repo facility exceeds an average of Rs. 10,000 crore, over say a fortnight or a month, it should trigger MSS or CRR action. In other words, the reverse repo should operate like a Plimsoll Line.

It is conceivable that all these measures would not suffice to tackle the capital inflows. In such a situation the authorities should use unorthodox measures like a 10 per cent unremunerated reserve requirement on capital inflows (excluding a few specific inflows like FDI) and the amount should be immobilised for a period of one year. The scheme should be carefully crafted, well in advance of its actual implementation, so as to avoid any snags which are inevitable if the scheme is hurriedly drawn up.

The avalanche of capital inflows cannot continue indefinitely. At some point of time, there will be an exodus of capital. If we do not undertake appropriate measures now we will pay a very heavy price in the future. The choice is very clear and the present call is for a strong and unswerving monetary policy.

Divya Bhaskar—October 15, 2007.

64 Long-Term Swings in Foreign Investment Policy

Equity versus Debt

The history of Indian foreign policy of the past hundred years is fascinating in terms of the various fundamental changes which have occurred over this long period.

In the period up to the 1930s there were little or no controls on the type of foreign investment, particularly from the sterling area. Foreign investors could freely choose the structure of their investments *viz.*, branch or subsidiaries. Also there were no controls on foreign debt.

With the onset of World War II and the emergence of exchange control there was some element of control, mainly for transactions from the dollar area.

After Independence, the Indian authorities started making meek noises on Indian participation in foreign companies. These noises became more strident in the 1960s and 1970s, culminating in the much dreaded Foreign Exchange Regulation Act (FERA).

A school of thought was developing in India that equity was massively expensive *vis-à-vis* debt, notwithstanding the technology transmission; the view emerging was that technology could always be separately bought (article in the *RBI Bulletin* by the present writer in 1966) and R.H. Patil's pioneering study of Japanese import of technology sans capital (1970). These studies were also supported in two unlikely quarters. First, Matthew J. Kust (an economist with the US Consulate) argued in his books and articles that US investment would move abroad only if the net of tax return was 20 per cent as against 10 per cent in the US domestic market. Another study by a UK academic, Michael Kidron, took a rather extreme stance that foreign capital in India had a predatory approach and that remittances out of India were manifold as compared with the actual capital inflow. The First Survey of Foreign Collaboration in Indian Industry (1969) provided significant information on capital inflows, outflows of remittances as also details of the pattern of technical collaboration agreements and restrictive clauses. More importantly, the official view was very apprehensive of foreign private capital and the balance tilted distinctly in favour of loan capital.

These trends became more focused in the 1970s and 1980s. International financial institutions and credit rating agencies argued, particularly in the period leading up to the 1990 balance of payments crisis, that foreign debt-GDP and debt-servicing ratios had climbed to unsustainable levels.

With the initiation of economic reforms, starting in 1991, there was a sea change. As part of significant liberalisation of foreign direct investment (FDI), foreign institutional investment (FII) was opened up in a big way. Fundamental taxation reform and easing of the overall regulatory framework made India an attractive destination for foreign equity investment. In contrast foreign investment in the government and corporate debt market is still not favoured by the authorities. This is partly attributable to the erroneous view that an exodus of foreign debt would disrupt markets and that any large equity outflows would be a self-punishment to the foreign investors in terms of market crashes and adverse movements in the exchange rate. In fact, however, given the magnitude of volatile foreign equity capital and volatile foreign debt capital, the logic would point to a larger detrimental impact if the equity capital were to exodus.

In an endeavour to encourage even larger equity capital inflows, the Indian authorities have been accommodative to anonymous investments through Participatory Notes (PNs). In the more recent period there has been some effort to curb the excesses of the PNs system. The issue has been widely debated and the authorities are undertaking a skilled operation of getting off the PNs escalator without any major damage.

The PNs issue is a problem of yesteryear and the authorities need to give attention to Private Equity (PE) and Venture Capital Funds (VCFs). It is not as if all these funds should be a taboo, but the authorities must fully understand the nature of these funds and ensure a transparent trail.

Now in all this foreign debt capital has become a poor cousin and it is time we bring about a better balance between the two types of foreign capital flows. The restrictions on market access for foreign debt funds and taxation need to be reviewed.

There is perhaps a need to undertake an independent analysis of the merits and demerits of private equity and debt flows and to work out a blend for optimising the two types of flows. It would also be necessary to work out detailed strategies for a large and sudden exodus of capital flows. There comes a time when a country has to fine tune its capital inflows. It is one thing for a defunct economist to recommend a 10 per cent unremunerated reserve requirement and quite another when a percipient Rahul Bajaj makes the same suggestion.

Divya Bhaskar—December 24, 2007.

VII

65 Gold

Nature's Gift to Small Savers

Every politician, every civil servant, every industrialist and every banker avers that gold is an evil and that small savers should stay away from this unproductive asset. The truth is all these venerated persons, without exception, hold piles of gold. The *aam aadmi* will buy gold, in jewellery form, on the occasions of birth, marriage and other auspicious dates.

Since 1991, the gold policy of the authorities has been liberalised but the purpose has been to satiate the public demand for jewellery. The powers that be still look down on gold as a pure investment avenue. This is most unfortunate as the *aam aadmi* is being duped into believing that as an investment avenue, gold is hazardous. Accordingly, little has been done to facilitate the holding of primary gold by small savers.

The liberalisation of gold and any facilities for convenience of trading in gold is stuck in the antiquated philosophy that liberalisation of the gold policy should wean small savers away from gold. The authorities should be neutral as regards consumer preferences as between gold and other durables.

Gold has been the safest instrument for saving and investment through the ages. Paper currency and stocks and shares are of relatively recent origin and have yet to prove themselves. The uniqueness of gold is that it does not deteriorate with age. While analysts warn that gold is presently at its highest level for 18 years, they fail to advise small investors that gold is the best hedge against inflation. Gold prices invariably move inversely to the value of currency. Thus, small savers would do well to hold a part of their assets in gold. What is being advocated is not that small savers buy jewellery, but that they should hold gold, preferably of 0.995 fineness in bars, biscuits or coins. The reason is that jewellery making and subsequent conversion into primary gold is very costly and almost a third of the gold value is lost.

Observers would no doubt tell us that banks are now selling gold coins, biscuits and bars. Experience does show that the *aam aadmi* does not really know where to buy primary gold. It is reported that a few banks—ICICI Bank, HDFC Bank, IndusInd Bank, Corporation Bank and a few others do sell gold to retail investors and are considering buyback facilities. The snag is most banks which provide demat facilities for shares and securities do not provide demat accounts in gold. Only one of the commodity exchanges provides demat facilities for larger holders of over one kg.

A bank which sells gold with a certificate on the fineness and weight can easily provide demat facilities. There may be problems of assaying and hallmarking if banks were to provide demat facilities for all gold including trinkets.

An important issue is gold should be available at a large number of banks so customers are not required to go to inconvenient locations. There is a glimmer of hope that the Central Warehousing Corporation (CWC) intends to set up facilities for storing gold at two locations in each state. Thank heavens for small mercies, but such facilities ought to be manifold.

The key to facilitating the meeting of small savers' demand for gold could be to provide demat facilities at competitive charges. It is reported that some safe custody charges for gold are as high as one per cent per annum plus 0.5 per cent as brokerage. A way out would be to allow the present share depository participants (DPs) who reportedly have 10 million demat accounts to demat gold which has all the safety requirement of certified hallmarking, standardisation and fineness and initially sold through banks. The DPs could in turn pass on the physical gold to a central agency akin to the NSDL. SEBI should not be averse to DPs undertaking demat of gold.

An incentive to demat gold could be that unlike physical holding of gold, demat gold could be exempted from wealth tax.

An issue can well be raised that it is hazardous for small savers to buy gold at today's high prices. Small savers have no way of predicting market peaks and troughs. What a small saver should consider is a systematic investment plan (SIP) for gold. This way the small saver reduces his price risk. Admittedly, a small saver should invest in gold essentially as a long-term investment.

Some analytical reports point to the strong possibility of gold prices rising sharply over the next three years, particularly if international inflation is not controlled. Central bank sellers may turn buyers.

There are clearly no guaranteed winners in investments. Small savers should diversify into gold in primary form. One fervently hopes that the authorities will provide the necessary infrastructure to facilitate investment in gold by small savers.

Divya Bhaskar—November 28, 2005.

66 Reserve Bank's Pot of Gold

The Reserve Bank of India (RBI) holds 358 tonnes of gold amounting to over US$ 5 billion or about 3.5 per cent of total foreign exchange reserves.

The RBI undertakes sophisticated analysis to decide the currency composition of the foreign currency reserves. But when it comes to official gold reserves, the RBI policy follows the three monkeys dictum: "see no evil, hear no evil, speak no evil". Such a policy is a sure way of loss maximisation. Should the RBI be indicted for this insensate policy? The unequivocal answer is a resounding 'no'. The blame clearly rests on the entire Indian polity which has totally erroneous preconceptions that the RBI should neither buy nor sell gold and that it should also not undertake gold-currency transactions. Such an ostrich-like approach results in major risk exposure. Advocates of the passive gold policy would no doubt claim that the value of gold reserves has gone up in the recent period. But such advocates conveniently forget that when gold prices fall, the RBI is a sitting duck waiting to be shot.

The US holds 60 per cent of its reserves in gold and the proportion is around 50 per cent for Germany, France, Italy and the Netherlands. Most central banks follow proactive gold policies with freedom to sell or buy gold. Although China and Japan hold a very small proportion of their reserves in gold, they are increasing the gold proportion. Again, Russia is on a decisive gold purchase spree. Under the central banks' agreement on gold, the member countries have agreed to limit sales up to 2009 to 2,500 tonnes or about 500 tonnes per year. Many of these countries are reconsidering their earlier stance of selling gold.

What should the Indian official gold policy be? The medium-term objective should be to hold say 10 per cent of the reserves in gold. This will imply that India should raise its gold holdings to around 1,100 tonnes. But we cannot expect the RBI to do this on its own. The Government should commission a high powered report on official gold holdings of the RBI and the report should be placed on the table of Parliament and after a comprehensive debate, the Government should formulate the broad contours of policy.

The authorities should work out a step-by-step policy. First, the RBI should be required to be transparent about the quality of its gold reserves. The RBI should indicate the proportion of its gold reserves in London Good Delivery Bars, other gold bars and trinkets. Hopefully, the proportion of trinkets in RBI's gold reserves should be sharply declining. These trinkets are sometimes alloys with a small proportion of other metals. A central bank just cannot afford to have any gold which is not London Good Delivery Bars.

Secondly, the Government should encourage the RBI to undertake locational swaps under which RBI swaps its trinkets and sub-standard bars for London Good Delivery Bars. This should be undertaken without any shipments of gold. The RBI can earn some interest on its gold holdings.

Thirdly, the RBI should be immediately empowered through legislative changes to undertake gold currency transactions and also undertake gold spot-forward transactions.

After the polity is sufficiently exposed to gold policy issues, the RBI should be encouraged to undertake outright gold purchases and sales up to say, 50 tonnes and on assessing the skills of the RBI, the amount can be gradually raised.

In the absence of a proactive policy, it must be understood that the present passive policy is very costly in terms of opportunities foregone. We entrust the RBI with management of foreign exchange assets of over US $ 135 billion. Should we not entrust the RBI to efficiently manage the gold reserves?

What is the outlook for international currencies? The Dollar, Euro, Yen and Sterling all have problems. This portends increased inflation and increase in gold prices in currency terms. There are forecasts that gold prices could rise beyond the 1983 peak of US $ 873 per ounce. Risk minimisation would warrant that central banks diversify their reserves.

The Indian polity has to make up its mind. Do we want to continue with the antiquated ostrich-like policy on gold and ignore the losses implicit in such a policy or are we willing to allow RBI to follow a sensible and active gold management policy?

Finally, is it not time to revive the idea of a Gold Bank which was mooted by the then Finance Minister, Dr. Manmohan Singh in his budget speech of February 1992? Or are we content with faulty analysis which resulted in an aborting of this novel idea? India is at the crossroads of gold policy and we have to decide between an insensate passive policy or a sensible modern proactive policy.

Divya Bhaskar—December 12, 2005.

67 Gold Exchange Traded Funds

A Bonanza for Retail Investors

In India, the official and intellectual approach to gold has all along been ambivalent. The posture of the powers that are closely aligned with Henry Ford's view that "Gold is the most useless thing in the world". Yet 10 per cent of the above ground world gold stocks are held in India.

In 1997, there was a major liberalisation of gold imports and Dr. Y.V. Reddy, the then Deputy Governor, was a key proponent of the liberalisation. Earlier, in 1991, the then Governor Mr. S. Venkitaramanan, mooted the idea of setting up a Gold Bank as a subsidiary of the RBI. In the Budget of February 1992, the then Finance Minister, Dr. Manmohan Singh, committed to the setting up of the Gold Bank. This was, however, aborted without transparently setting out the reasons for the *volte face*.

In a pathbreaking development, in 2007, Gold Exchange Traded Funds (GETF) were set up in India. The first GETF in the world was set up in 1993 and a total of US dollars 13 billion is invested in these instruments in different countries.

A GETF is an open-ended mutual fund which enables small retail investors to invest in gold in a dematerialised form without actually taking delivery of gold. The GETF mimics physical gold and the units of the GETF are traded on the stock exchanges. These schemes provide a retail investor a return close to the returns provided by physical gold. The GETF is not expected to outperform gold. Each unit of the GETF approximately represents one gram of gold. A retail investor can subscribe to a New Fund Offer (NFO) or buy into the GETF in the secondary market. The NFO carries with it an entry load while the secondary market purchase would be subject to brokerage charges. While purchases from the NFO would be subject to a stipulated minimum number of units, the secondary market purchase could be as small as one unit i.e., one gram of gold.

An essential feature of the GETF, from the viewpoint of the retail investor, is that the investor holds units and can, at any time, sell the units at a price which approximates the value of gold at the time of sale. This obviates the drawbacks of physical gold, such as storage, liquidity and purity. The GETFs are free from wealth tax and are not subject to the securities transactions tax; they are, subject to capital gains tax.

What are the prospects of GETFs in India? One-third of the world demand for gold for investment purposes comes from India and this provides a very large catchment area for GETFs in India. The Benchmark GETF raised Rs. 100 crore and the UTI GETF raised Rs. 250 crore. The GETFs hold a great potential in India and a number of funds are in the queue—Tata, ICICI Prudential, Kotak, Escorts and Reliance. Furthermore, Optmix (ING Group) has prepared a prospectus for a Gold Fund-of-Funds scheme. DSP Merrill Lynch is proposing a fund for overseas investments by residents in world mining companies. Thus, there are interesting vistas in India for retail investors in gold. GETFs provide an avenue for diversification of assets by retail investors. Investments in GETFs will not outperform equities but the gold price cycle is different from the roller coaster of the equity market. Retail investors would do well to allocate say 5 per cent of their portfolio to GETFs.

What is the international outlook for gold? Gold is the ultimate dollar hedge. The US dollar could weaken for a number of reasons. First, countries heavily invested in the US dollar could dump the dollar. Secondly, there could be sharp increases in oil prices. Thirdly, the US trade and budget deficits could eventually reflect in a weakening of the dollar. Paul Walker, CEO of the Gold Fields Market Survey, claims that in the near term the price of gold could rise from US dollar 670 per ounce to US dollar 800 per ounce. Marc Faber, the investment guru, recommends gold as a safe investment option. Over the long run gold has the potential for a compound annual rate of growth of 9 per cent

Most central banks actively manage their gold portfolio, yet the RBI is forced by the polity to follow a totally passive "Do Nothing" policy which is the surest way of losing money. Russia is contemplating raising its official gold from 500 tonnes to 1100 tonnes (Russia produces about 200 tonnes of gold per annum). There is talk about China increasing its official stocks from 600 tonnes to 2,500 tonnes. The least the RBI could do is to undertake a comprehensive external examination of the role of gold in RBI reserves with lessons drawn from other central banks. The policy options should be put in the public domain. The polity must own up to its responsibility and must realise the heavy losses inflicted on the RBI by the insensate ostrich-like passive gold management policy.

Divya Bhaskar—April 16, 2007.

VIII

68 Corporate Social Responsibility and the Knocking on the Window

Put in very simple terms, corporate social responsibility is defined in the literature as the ethical behaviour of a company towards society. In India, the role of corporate social responsibility has been gaining momentum over the past decade, though there are some cases of corporates which have all along shown a great deal of sensitivity to social responsibility.

It is increasingly being realised that it is in the interest of the corporate sector to accept social responsibility. In the debate on profits *versus* philanthropy, it is sometimes naively argued that profit is more important as without profit there can be no philanthropy; in effect it is argued that unless people have, how can they give.

We now live in an avaricious society wherein the greater the wealth, the greater your standing in society. Witness the Great Annual Derby race in the financial press to show who are the richest corporate heads. Social responsibility for once can be forgotten; we worship the biggest plutocrats and ultimately in the present day this is what counts.

This is in no way to denigrate what a number of prominent corporates have done by way of fulfilling their social responsibility. While comparisons are odious, names which readily come to mind are Tatas, Wipro, Infosys and Reliance. This is not to say that a large number of other corporates are not fulfilling their corporate social responsibility. Corporates are increasingly recognising that profits and social responsibility are not mutually exclusive; in fact, they are mutually reinforcing. But the sad truth is that most corporates are content to put by into socially desired channels a certain proportion of their profits and thus salve their conscience.

A provocative small pamphlet by Arun Maira, Chairman, Boston Consulting Group should be made mandatory reading for all Chief Executive

Officers (CEOs). Arun Maira recounts the parable of "The Knocking on the Window." Ten to twenty years ago, the privileged segments of society travelled in un-air-conditioned cars; at that time the poor and beggars could be ignored. But now people drive in air-conditioned cars and the knocking on the window has become furious and those inside the cars can no longer ignore the fury and what it portends for the future—unless things change drastically.

Maira argues that across the corporate spectrum the catchword is downsizing which does not fit into the knocking on the window.

While the present model stresses efficiency and increased productivity as the route for the trickling down effect to alleviate poverty, Maira fears that the political system cannot hold on to the slogan of privatisation unless it shows demonstrative benefits for the poor. Donating money for social causes may appear to release corporates of their responsibilities but such initiatives are clearly insufficient.

Maira asserts that there is a need for a new business model wherein corporates engage a large number of poor people as agents rather than employees. Not only will incomes of the poor rise but the poor will become bigger consumers and thus contribute to corporate growth. The relationships among a large number of parties should work on commercial lines rather than as a charity.

The poor will honour their debts if their contracts are fair. The underprivileged are shown to be reliable business partners. We often talk of the Grameen Bank of Bangladesh but banks in Mumbai are oblivious of the remarkable lending efforts of a Mumbai businessman who lends to street children and the recovery rate is good.

Maira persuasively argues that we have to answer the knocking on the window and for this we need a new management textbook. The "e-choupal" model of ITC is a promising start.

The knocking on the window is a warning for corporate honcho but it is also an opportunity, provided management does not use traditional lenses. The new pathways provide profits for both corporates and the poor.

Arun Maira has provided a signal service and one hopes that this small pamphlet is not only read by CEOs but the public at large. It would be no exaggeration to say that Arun Maira has provided the mainsprings for a new and viable business model.

The haves and the have-nots are at the crossroads. They have a choice here and now between going on the confrontationist path or the path of a fruitful and enduring partnership. Let us hope that sanity will prevail and Maira's seminal work will not be in vain.

Divya Bhaskar—January 23, 2006.

69 RBI Balance Sheet

Mirror Image of the Economy

The Annual Report of the Reserve Bank of India (RBI) 2006-07 was released on August 30, 2007. Unknown to most readers is the valuable insight provided by the RBI Accounts and Balance Sheet.

The RBI is very different from a corporate enterprise. Its performance cannot be judged by its profits or losses. If profits swell it does not mean that the economy is in the pink of health; in fact it could reflect inappropriate macro policies.

One has to disentangle the transaction of the sale of RBI's stake in the State Bank of India (SBI). The RBI sold its 59.73 per cent stake in SBI at Rs. 35,531 crore and, net of its purchase price of Rs. 1,223 crore, it transferred Rs. 34,308 crore to the government as profit. In effect, the government got the stake in SBI virtually free of cost. It is unfortunate that this transaction is justified on the basis of the Narasimham Committee II recommendation that regulators should not be owners. This is a distortion of the Narasimham Committee II recommendation by the RBI Internal Group (2001). The Committee did not recommend that the RBI should sell its stake in SBI to government, which is an even bigger regulator. Narasimham II recommended that both RBI and government should reduce their stake in public sector banks to 33 per cent. Quite properly, the RBI proceeds of the sale of its stake in SBI should have been put into the RBI's Reserve Fund.

Nowhere does the opening up of the economy show more visibly than in the RBI Balance Sheet. Of the total assets of about Rs. 10 lakh crore, foreign assets are equivalent to 86 per cent of the total. Domestic assets, largely government debt to the RBI, are now insignificant, reflecting a move away from central banking financing of the government. It is the external sector which determines the movements in the RBI Balance Sheet. We can no longer claim to be a closed economy and developments in the international economy will have a serious impact on the economy. We are warned that, in future we will be quickly punished for inappropriate macro policies.

In the year ended June 30, 2007, the RBI's return on average domestic assets was 5.3 per cent while its earning on average foreign assets was 4.6 per cent. In the year ended June 30, 2006, the return on domestic assets was only 1.8 per cent as the RBI incurred large sterilisation costs under the reverse repo (where in the RBI absorbs excess liquidity). In the year ended June 2007 such absorption under the reverse repo was subject to a very low ceiling for part of the year.

The RBI has a Currency and Gold Revaluation Reserve which absorbs the fluctuations in exchange rates. This reserve fell from Rs. 86,789 crore in June 2006 to Rs. 21,724 crore in June 2007, or equivalent to only 2.8 per cent of total foreign assets. The RBI does have a Contingency and Asset Development Reserve and the Reserve Fund which, taken together with the Currency and Gold Revaluation Reserve, amounts to 13 per cent of the total foreign assets. In other words, the RBI would be completely wiped out if the rupee were to appreciate, *vis-à-vis* major currencies by a further 13 per cent.

There is a whole range of literature on central bank losses. More often than not, the central bank losses are reflective of inappropriate exchange rate policies. If a country appreciates its currency beyond what is warranted by fundamentals it will reflect in large losses for the central bank. Rare is the instance where a government publicly, and in advance, underwrites such losses (Germany was a notable exception). Provision of exchange rate guarantees, payment of high interest on cash balances of banks with the central bank and issue of central bank bonds are sure ways of incurring large losses. There are cases of central banks going bankrupt (the Philippines). Let this be a warning for the enthusiasts of appreciation of the rupee.

Advocates of an appreciation of the rupee should pause and think. Building sound institutions is difficult and wrong policies should not be allowed to decimate the RBI. To the extent that there is an avalanche of capital inflows in say, the next six or nine months, the RBI should actively use the Market Stabilisation Scheme (MSS) and the cash reserve ratio

(CRR) and other administrative/monetary/fiscal measures to manage the net capital flows. The high priests in the temple of money should not fight shy of defending their faith which is well grounded in sound macroeconomic realities.

Divya Bhaskar—September 17, 2007

70 The Tragedy of Pulses

India's Shame

When petroleum prices rise, there is much din in the media. When wheat, rice and edible oil prices rise, there is enough uproar to the discomfort to the government of the day. When overall prices rise, the government gets its act together. But there is a silent tragedy affecting large tracts of the population, yet there is no murmur. This relates to the vital question of the output, consumption and prices of pulses. The wheat and rice revolutions got rid of the problem of periodic shortages. We have the white revolution which brought about major improvements in the production and distribution of milk. We have the Technology Mission on Oilseeds to take care of deficits in edible oils. But whatever happened to the Technology Mission on Pulses? This seems to have fallen by the wayside. Between 1950-51 and 2001, rice output rose from 20 million tonnes to 85 million tonnes, wheat output rose from 6 million tonnes to 70 million tonnes, but pulses rose from 8 million tonnes to only 11 million tonnes. The area and yields for rice and wheat have risen sharply but for pulses it has been stagnant.

Why should we be concerned about pulses? Pulses are the single most important source of protein consumption in India. From an output of 14 million tonnes in 1990-91 there have been sharp year to year fluctuations but other than in one year, *viz.*, 2003-04, when output was 15 million tonnes, the output has not exceeded the 1990-91 level, and in fact it has been lower in most years. With the rising population it is clear that per capita consumption has fallen, particularly among the weakest segments of society.

In some quarters there is a false sense of complacency. After all we have McDonald's and Kentucky Fried Chicken, so what if pulses output stagnates! But really we should have a national conscience. Vast tracts of the population are dependent on pulses as their only source of protein and for many years, large segments of the population have been denied any source of protein.

We have foreign exchange pouring out of our ears so why cannot we just import pulses? There are two reasons why this is not possible. First, the supplies in the world are just not sufficient—we can import chick peas (*chola*) but our standard pulses *viz.*, *urad*, *moong*, *tur* and *masur* are just not available. Secondly, although soyabean meal is available in plenty, and it is the best source of protein, insufficient efforts have been made to popularise its consumption.

Now what needs to be done? First the government should be serious about the Pulses Technology Mission and be prepared to provide resources for bringing about a quantum jump in output. Secondly, while fiscal purists would be against any subsidy for pulses, there could be a very small shift from rice and wheat subsidies to pulses to ensure that pulses are provided to the weaker segments at affordable prices. In the case of pulses, we should be willing to shed our inhibitions about corporate entry into agriculture and the government should provide incentives to ensure that this vital gap in protein supplies is removed.

There should be a major campaign to popularise texturised soyabean meal; the beauty of this product is its neutral flavour and it can take on the flavour of any vegetable or condiment. If, over the years, we could bring about a quantum jump in the consumption of wheat in the southern states it should surely be possible to pupularise the consumption of soyabean meal.

We talk so much about benign inflation. Does anyone care to give attention to the fact that in 2005-06 the increase in prices of pulses was 33 per cent and, together with the sharp increases of earlier years, pulses are rapidly going out of the food basket of large tracts of the population? Prices of pulses in the current financial year 2006-07 have hit through the roof and India is on the verge of a major pulses crisis, yet there seems to be total complacency.

If we want to ensure a healthy population, the government should step up efforts to ensure higher production of pulses. The pulses problem has been neglected for a very long period and a government committed to the welfare of the *aam aadmi* should use unorthodox measures to resolve the pulses shortage. It is India's shame that it supplies technology to the rest of the world but cannot tackle the problem of protein deficiency in mass tracts of its own population. In the absence of concerted action, the pulses tragedy could boomerang on the entire nation. India's shame must be erased.

Divya Bhaskar—October 16, 2006.

Index